GETTING A GRIP

ALSO BY FRANCES MOORE LAPPÉ

Democracy's Edge: Choosing to Save Our Country
by Bringing Democracy to Life

You Have the Power: Choosing Courage in a Culture of Fear
(with Jeffrey Perkins)

Hope's Edge: The Next Diet for a Small Planet (with Anna Lappé)

The Quickening of America:
Rebuilding Our Nation, Remaking Our Lives (with Paul Martin Du Bois)

Diet for a Small Planet

Taking Population Seriously (with Rachel Schurman)

Rediscovering America's Values

Betraying the National Interest (with Rachel Schurman and Kevin Danaher)

World Hunger: Twelve Myths (with Joseph Collins, Peter Rosset and Luis Esparza)

What To Do After You Turn Off the T.V.

Nicaragua: What Difference Could a Revolution Make? (with Joseph Collins and Paul Rice)

Now We Can Speak (with Joseph Collins)

Aid as Obstacle (with Joseph Collins and David Kinley)

Mozambique and Tanzania: Asking the Big Questions (with Adele Beccar-Varela)

Food First: Beyond the Myth of Scarcity (with Joseph Collins and Cary Fowler)

FRANCES MOORE LAPPÉ

GETTING A GRIP

clarity, creativity, and courage in a world gone mad

Social benefit organizations are encouraged to contact us about bulk discounts for their constituencies.

Richard R. Rowe, Publisher

Printed in the United States by Grossman Marketing Group, a GCC/IBT Union member

Distributed by Chelsea Green Publishing
First printing, October 2007

10 9 8 7 6 5 4 3 2 1

This book is printed with soy ink on acid-free recycled paper.

Publisher's Cataloging in Publication Data

Lappé, Frances Moore.
    Getting a grip : clarity, creativity and courage in a world gone mad / by Frances Moore Lappé.
    p. cm.
    Includes bibliographical references and index.
    ISBN-13: 978-0-9794142-4-4
    ISBN-10: 0-9794142-4-5

    1. Social participation. 2. Democracy.
    3. Sustainable development   I. Title.

        HN65.L37 2007   361.2
                                 QBI07-600186

Small Planet Media
25 Mt. Auburn St., Ste. 203
Cambridge, MA 02138
(617) 441-6300 x115
www.smallplanetmedia.org

For RRR and the
conversation that never ends

GETTING A GRIP

clarity, creativity, and courage in a world gone mad

Acknowledgements xi
Opening Note. xiii

CLARITY

1 The Straightjacket 3

   peeling away the layers 5

   elections plus a market…that's democracy? 8

   lizzie's lessons 9

   thin democracy's pitfalls 11

   deeper dangers 14

   humility and hope 18

2 New Eyes 21

   goodness *of* or *in* human nature? 25

   an ecology of democracy: five qualities 29

   a premise of plenty, a spiral of hope 37

3 What Democracy Feels Like 41

   nine dimensions: some glimpses 42

   why now? four revolutions. 63

CREATIVITY

4 Power Invisible. 73
   one choice we don't have. 74
   mirrors in our brains 75
   power isn't a four-letter word 78
   relational power's under-appreciated sources 80
   drops count 83

5 The Art of Power 85
   democracy's arts 87
   the power of simply listening 88
   conflict as creative 91
   kids learn conflict is okay. 94

6 Talking Democracy. 97
   globalization or global corporate power? 98
   free market-free trade or fair market-fair trade? 99
   regulations or standards? 101
   consumers or buyers? 101

COURAGE

7   Seize the Moment 109

    a downward spin 110

    a rude shock 113

8   When Fear Means Go 117

    fear as pure energy 119

    fear and conflict 120

    as it is 123

    old thoughts, new thoughts 125

    inner applause 126

9   Sanity in Motion 129

    claiming our sanity 130

    protection 133

    a cautionary tale, the danger of good intentions 135

    on issues versus entry points 136

    an internal checklist 150

    bold humility 153

    knowing 154

    An Invitation 156
    Questions to Spark Talk and Action 157
    Recommended Reading .169
    Endnotes 173
    Index 179
    Books from the Small Planet Insitute 187

IDEAS

to help us probe deeply, identify causal forces,
choose entry points, and shift patterns

IDEA 1: Thin Democracy vs. Living Democracy. 24

IDEA 2: We All Have Public Lives. 36

IDEA 3: Rethinking Power 78

IDEA 4: Ten Arts of Democracy. 88

IDEA 5: Toward a Language of Democracy 103

IDEA 6: The Inner World of Living Democracy 112

IDEA 7: Seven Ways to Rethink Fear. .127

IDEA 8: Living Democracy's Checklist .153

ACKNOWLEDGEMENTS

This book reflects a life's quest, so by rights I should acknowledge everybody who's influenced my path. But if I were to make good on that thought, this little book would be huge. So I've tried to restrain myself.

First, I thank Richard Rowe, my partner, for the joy of our common exploration and your countless selfless acts of support enabling this book. Likewise, my children Anthony and Anna Lappé, whose encouragement and advice, as always, kept me going. At the Small Planet Institute, I am grateful for Jess Wilson's cheerful determination as she deftly managed the many dimensions of bringing forth this, the first Small Planet Media production. Thank you Mark Douglass, Small Planet Media Marketing Director, for your creative, steady, and tireless effort. Matthew Morrissey's diligent research and supportive presence consistently smoothed the way. Zoë Rosenfeld's insightful editorial assistance and the careful copyediting of Kate Tighe and Shveta Thakrar made this work more readable.

I'm indebted to Jeffrey Perkins for collaborating on our book, *You Have the Power,* which fed my chapter here on transforming fear. Thank you, my manuscript readers, who offered feedback improving this book: Diana Beliard, Gloria Foster, Ephraim Julius Freed, Michael Richardson, Walter Robb, Laura Shelton, and Jim Staton. Our Institute's TeamDemocracy members offered a range of support for which I'm grateful. They include: Carolina Aparicio, Noah Joffe-Halpern, Michael Kowalski, Keith Lane, Erica Licht, Rebecca Mailman, Dani O'Brien, and Angela Smalley.

For the book's interior design, thank you Chad Morgan; for its cover, Amy Hayes. For helping us spread this message, I thank Dorie Clark and the Mainstream Media Project. At Chelsea Green Publishing, thank you Margo Baldwin, Mike Dyer, Peg O'Donnell, Kalen Landow, and the rest of your team for your enthusiastic embrace of this project.

Friends especially supportive of this effort include Diana Beliard, Rose Pritzker, Linda Pritzker, Aaron Stern, Mark Finser, Josh Mailman, Hathaway Barry and Susan Kanaan.

Finally, two sources of inspiration: I am indebted to the Industrial Areas Foundation for your leadership in developing concepts of power and public life that have so shaped my thinking, and to my friends at the Unitarian-Universalist Service Committee for creating "covenant group" guides based on my *Democracy's Edge.* Your initiative was the spark that led me to imagine this book.

OPENING NOTE
GETTING MY GRIP

've finally figured it out. I am not overwhelmed, depressed, confused, or bewildered by our world gone mad. I'm ready. I'm *past* ready.

I just want to go for it.

Why can't we have a nation—why can't we have a *world* we're proud of? Why can't we stop wringing our hands over poverty, hunger, species decimation, genocide, and death from curable disease that we know is all needless? The truth is there is no reason we can't.

They say—whoever the "they" are—that as we age, we mellow. I don't think so. I'm getting less and less patient.

Why? Because I realize that humanity has no excuses anymore. In the span of my own lifetime, both historical evidence and breakthroughs in knowledge have wiped out all our excuses.

We know that we know how to end this needless suffering, and we have all the resources to do it. From sociology and anthropology to economics, from education and ecology to systems analysis... the evidence is in. We know what works.

"Soft" psychology as well as "hard" neuroscience also confirm that we humans come equipped with a moral compass—with deep needs and sensibilities that make us yearn to end the suffering. Yet we deny these feelings every single day at huge cost to our society and to our world.

No physical obstacle is stopping us. Nothing. The barrier is in our heads. We are creating this world gone mad, not because we're compelled to by some deep flaws in our nature and not because Nature itself is stingy and unforgiving, but because of ideas we hold. *Ideas?*

Yes. This is one of the most startling discoveries—awakenings—of the last century: Human beings are in fact creatures of the mind. Our ideas about reality determine what we see, what we believe is possible, and therefore what we become. And we also now know that human beings can change our core, life-shaping ideas, even our ideas of democracy, of power, of fear, and—yes—of evil itself.

As we do, we no longer have to settle for grasping at straws—wild acts of protest, or tearful acts of charity, or any other short-term, feel-less-bad steps. We become open to the possibility of real change, And, when you think about it, how could we ever believe "the world" can change unless we experience ourselves changing?

So this little book is about learning to see the killer ideas that trap us and letting them go. It's about people in all walks of life interrupting the spiral of despair and reversing it with new ideas, ingenious innovation—and courage. It's about finding that mixture of anger and hope to energize us for this do-or-die effort. Why not go for it?

—Frances Moore Lappé
Cambridge, May 2007

PART 1
CLARITY

1 THE STRAIGHTJACKET

*Why are we as societies creating a
world that we as individuals abhor?*

This is the question that's propelled my life for decades now.

It *is* really bewildering. We know that no human being actually gets up in the morning vowing, "Yeah, today I'm going to make sure another child dies needlessly of hunger," or muttering, "Sure, I'll do my part to heat the planet and obliterate entire species."

Yet each day over twenty-five thousand young children die of hunger and poverty, and roughly one hundred more species are forever gone. And the crises are not abating; they just keep whacking us: global climate chaos, terrorism, racial and religious divides, life-stunting poverty, pandemic disease…and now our own government's betrayal of constitutional principle.

Again…*why?*

I think for a lot of us, there is no real answer. Things just keep happening. We know *we're* not in control, and it seems like nobody is.

Sure, some people believe the problem is just us—human beings are just screwed up. Whether you call it original sin or simple selfishness, it's just who we are. Others are more targeted in assigning blame. For them, the root cause of our planet's crises is those *particular* people…the evil ones. Osama bin Laden, George W. Bush, Saddam Hussein, Dick Cheney. Still others believe we have no choice. We must conform to the now-proven economic laws of the global marketplace or suffer an even worse fate.

For all their many differences, the consequences of these views are similar. They leave us powerless. With no grip on how things got so bad, we have no clue as to where to start to correct them. So we're tempted to seize on any gesture of charity or any burst of protest—any random act of sanity. For a moment, at least, we can feel less useless in the face of the magnitude of the crises. Ultimately, though, acts of desperation contribute to our despair if we're unable to link our specific acts to real solutions.

Feeling powerless, we're robbed of energy and creativity, with hearts left open to fear and depression. No wonder the World Health Organization tells us depression is now the fourth leading cause of lost productive life worldwide—expected to jump to second place in fifteen years. Or that suicides worldwide now exceed homicides by 50 percent.[1]

But what if…what if…together with our friends, family, and acquaintances, we could probe the root causes of the biggest threats to our planet? What if we were able to grasp something of the common origins of these threats and then identify powerful entry points to interrupt them? And more than that, what if we could then feel we are shifting the destructive underlying patterns toward health?

Now, that's power. Our power.

PEELING AWAY THE LAYERS

Over the years, I've come to sense that blaming the evil other stumbles on what logicians call an attribution error, the misplaced identification of cause. And it's a pretty serious error, for it releases us from asking really helpful questions: What is it about the current order we ourselves are creating that elicits so much pain and destruction? And peeling to the next layer: What are our own unexamined assumptions and beliefs that leave us feeling so powerless?

In the late nineteenth century, for example, Indians outnumbered the British civil servants ruling them by three hundred thousand to one.[2] Yet Indians' widespread belief in their powerlessness continued until Gandhi and others re-framed reality, revealing the power that was theirs all along. In 1930, Indians declared independence and, sparked by Gandhi's example, thousands walked over two hundred miles to the sea to protest the British salt tax. Within seventeen years, the Indian people had ousted their colonial rulers.

It's pretty easy to see how mental concepts—ideas about reality—disempower others, whether it's a belief in a ruler's "divine right" or a conviction about the inferiority of a lower caste. It's much harder to perceive the mental straightjackets we ourselves don every day.

Our future, though, may well depend on giving it a try.

In *The Anatomy of Human Destructiveness,* social philosopher Eric Fromm observes that all human beings carry within us "frames of orientation" through which we make sense of the world. They determine—often literally—what we can see, what we believe humans are made of, and therefore what we believe is possible. In other words, just about everything.

Now this trait might be just fine…*if* our frames are life-serving, but, Fromm warns, they aren't always. To stir us to realize the danger within this unique aspect of our humanness—our filtering through socially determined frames—Fromm came up with this mind-bending declaration: "It is man's humanity that makes him so inhuman."[3]

Cultures live or die, Fromm is telling us, not by violence, or by chance, but ultimately by ideas. And unfortunately for our precious planet, much of the world appears locked within sets of ideas, including our ideas about democracy, that actually contribute to our "inhumanity"—whether that means inflicting or ignoring the suffering and loss mounting worldwide.

Inside the front cover, please see what I call a *Spiral of Powerlessness.* It is the scary current of limiting beliefs and consequences in which I sense we're trapped.

Its premise is "lack."

There isn't enough of anything, neither enough "goods"— whether jobs or jungles—nor enough "goodness" because human beings are, well, pretty bad. These ideas have been drilled into us for centuries, as world religions have dwelt on human frailty, and Western political ideologies have picked up similar themes.

"*Homo homini lupus* [we are to one another as wolves]," wrote the influential seventeenth-century philosopher Thomas Hobbes. Repeating a Roman aphorism—long before we'd learned how social wolves really are—Hobbes reduced us to cutthroat animals.

Private interest...is the only immutable point in the human heart.
—ALEXIS DE TOCQUEVILLE, *DEMOCRACY IN AMERICA*, 1835[4]

From that narrow premise, it follows that it's best to mistrust deliberative problem-solving, distrust even democratic government, and grasp for an infallible law—the market!—driven by the only thing we can really count on, human selfishness. From there, wealth concentrates and suffering increases, confirming the dreary premises that set the spiral in motion in the first place.

What this downward spiral tells me is that we humans now suffer from what linguists call "hypocognition," the lack of a critical concept we need to thrive. And it's no trivial gap! Swept into the vortex of this destructive spiral, we're missing an understanding of democracy vital and compelling enough to create the world we want.

Democracy? Why start there?

Democracy is *the* problem-solving device much of the world now embraces as the way to meet common needs and solve common problems. So if our definition of democracy is flawed, we are in big trouble.

ELECTIONS PLUS A MARKET...THAT'S DEMOCRACY?

To see what's missing, let's explore a bit more the dominant conception of reality in which our nation's culture, especially our view of democracy, is grounded. As just noted, its foundational premise is scarcity—there just isn't enough of *anything*—from love to jobs to parking spots. In such a world, only one type of person thrives. So if you peel away all the fluff, humans must have evolved as competitive materialists, elbowing one another out in a giant scramble over scarce stuff.

Absorbing this shabby caricature of humanity, we understandably see ourselves as incapable of making a success of democratic deliberation—assuming a selfish nature, we're sure somebody will always muck it up. Not to fret, though. We've been assured with ever-greater intensity since the 1980s that if real democracy—deliberating together to shape a common purpose and strategies—is suspect, there's a perfect solution: Just turn over our fate to an impersonal law that will settle things for us. Privatize and commoditize all that we can—from health care to prison management to schools—in order to take full advantage of what Ronald Reagan called "the magic of the market."

And government? It's something done *to* us or *for* us by taking "our money," so the less of it the better.

From these assumptions, it is easy to see why most Americans grow up absorbing the notion that democracy boils down to just two things—elected government and a market economy. Since in the United States we have both, there isn't much for us to do except show up at the polls and shop.

I like to call this stripped-down duo Thin Democracy because it is feeble.

We breathe in this definition like invisible ether, so it's easy to jump over an unpleasant fact: Real democracy and our peculiar variant of a market economy are based on opposing principles. Democracy derives from the Greek: *demos* (people) plus *kratos* (rule). Thus democracy depends on the wide dispersion of power so that each citizen has both a vote and a voice. But our particular market economy, driven by one rule—that is, highest return to shareholder and corporate chiefs—moves inexorably in the opposite direction. By continually returning wealth to wealth, a one-rule economy leads to an ever-increasing concentration of power.

LIZZIE'S LESSONS

In the early 1900s, Lizzie Maggie tried to warn us. Lizzie was a concerned Quaker, worried that one-rule capitalism would do us in. So she came up with a board game she hoped would entertain us but also serve as an object lesson: It may take all night, but the rules of the game eventually drive property into the hands of one player, ending the fun for everybody.

Well, Lizzie's idea got into the hands of Parker Brothers. They called it Monopoly, and the rest, as they say, is history—history that, in this case, reveals just what Maggie was trying to tell us about one-rule economics. Just five companies sell well over half of all toys in America.[5] More generally, in 1955, sales of the top five hundred corporations equaled one-third of the U.S. gross domestic product. They now account for two-thirds.[6]

As corporate wealth concentrates, so does private: Here in the United States, between 1979 and 2001, family income among the wealthiest 5 percent leapt by 81 percent, but families in the bottom 20 percent saw virtually no gain.[7] The gap separating America's average CEO's compensation and average worker's pay has widened tenfold in a generation, so today the CEO earns as much by lunchtime on the first day of the year as a minimum wage worker earns the entire year.[8]

In the United States over the last four years, the share of economic growth going to corporate profits increased by over two-thirds, while the share rewarding workers fell, even as their productivity continued to rise.[9] Today America's biggest employer, Wal-Mart, pays its workers in inflation-adjusted dollars only 40 percent as much as the biggest employer in 1969, GM, paid its employees—not to mention the workers' benefits now stripped away.[10]

For the first time, the four hundred richest Americans are all billionaires, with combined wealth of $1.25 trillion, roughly comparable to the total annual income of half the world's people. Worldwide, the number of billionaires is exploding. Growing eight times faster than the global economy, it is now at 946 people with a total wealth almost 40 percent greater than the entire GDP of China.[11]

So we didn't learn from Lizzie. We didn't get it—that to keep the game going, we citizens have to devise rules to ensure that wealth continually circulates. Otherwise, it all ends up in one player's pile. (In my household, it was usually my brother's!)

Yet under the spell of one-rule economics, most economists ignore this truth, as well as new jaw-dropping evidence that markets, by themselves, don't create livable societies:

Worldwide, during the 1990s, every one hundred dollars in economic growth reduced the poverty of the world's billion poorest people by just *sixty pennies.*[12]

Denial runs so deep, though, that the pro-corporate British journal, *The Economist*, apparently with a straight face, can describe inequality deepening worldwide as a "snag" in the system.[13] And well-meaning academics, with Columbia University's Jeffrey Sachs in the lead, can rally us to end global poverty by exporting our assumed-to-be successful economic model to them.[14]

So we remain blind to Thin Democracy's pitfalls.

THIN DEMOCRACY'S PITFALLS

Death to open markets. Despite the myth of competitive capitalism, writes economist James Galbraith, "[C]orporations exist to control markets and often to replace them."[15] Two companies have succeeded in controlling roughly three-fourths of the global grain trade[16]; one, Monsanto, accounts for 88 percent of the area planted worldwide with genetically modified seed and/or seed with biotech traits. Six corporations control most global media, from publishing to movies, and five control almost two-thirds of U.S. gasoline sales.[17]

In our one-rule economy, concentrated economic power is inevitable, destroying the very open, competitive market that was the rationale for the whole set-up to begin with. Wasn't it? Competitive, fair markets cannot be sustained, it turns out, outside of a genuinely democratic polity.

Just as with the protection of civil liberties, open markets depend on *us*, on our creating and continually monitoring rules that keep them open. Corporations want the opposite; they seek control over markets to ensure highest returns—not because they're run by bad people, but because the rules we've set up encourage them to.

History bears out this truth: it was only when Americans did step up to the plate, especially in the period from 1933 to 1945, and created fairness rules—including the right of workers to organize, Social Security, and a legal minimum wage—that our country experienced a dramatic narrowing of the gap between most of us and a tiny minority at the top.[18] The approach fostered broad-based economic prosperity for decades: Our median family income grew four times faster between 1947 and 1973 than it has since—as America has forsaken Lizzie's commonsense insight.[19]

Unfortunately, Thin Democracy's pitfalls don't stop here.

Warping of politics. Concentrated economic power, flowing inevitably from a one-rule economy, ends up infecting and warping our political system, as well. Sixty-one lobbyists now walk the corridors of power in Washington, D.C., for every one person we citizens have elected to represent our interests there.[20]

[T]he liberty of a democracy is not safe if the people tolerate the growth of private power to the point where it becomes stronger than their democratic state itself. That, in its essence, is fascism...

—FRANKLIN DELANO ROOSEVELT, 1938[21]

When citizens are outnumbered sixty-one to one, private power supersedes public power—as FDR warned us seven decades ago. Little wonder! To pick just a few frightening examples:

- for almost six years after 9/11, the chemical industry lobby was able to resist measures needed to secure fifteen thousand chemical plants against attack.[22]
- while five thousand Americans die annually from food-borne illnesses, the food industry is able to block mandatory recalls.[23]
- ex-oil lobbyist Philip Cooney was so tight with the Bush White House that he edited official reports to downplay climate change.[24]
- pharmaceutical lobbyists helped craft a healthcare law that forbids Medicare to negotiate drug prices—while we pay double what Europeans do for identical drugs.

So more and more Americans feel their democracy has been stolen, and they know by whom. Ninety percent of us agree that corporations have too much influence in Washington.[25]

DEEPER DANGERS

More than unworkable, Thin Democracy is dangerous. The power it gives corporations to put their own short-term gain ahead of our survival is only one danger.

The fragility of centralized power. Contrary to lessons drummed into us, concentrated power is often not resilient, efficient, or smart. The Inca and the Aztecs, huge civilizations, fell to conquistadors in no time, while the leaderless, decentralized Apaches fended off harsh attacks for two centuries.[26] Concentrated power often isolates itself and thus fails to learn. Think only of the, "I'm in the decider" bunker stance of the Bush White House that led the U.S. into Iraq, one of our country's most horrific foreign policy blunders.

Missing problem solvers. The flipside is that the centralized power of Thin Democracy leaves most of us feeling powerless, robbing the planet of just the problem solvers we most need. It encourages us to look to the "market" or to CEOs or to government higher-ups for answers, but our planet's problems are too complex, pervasive, and interconnected to be addressed from the top down. Solutions depend on the insights, experience, and ingenuity of people most affected—all thwarted when citizens are cut out and manipulated, and when decisions get made secretly by the few.

Put slightly differently, solutions require in-the-moment inventiveness and widespread behavior changes, and both depend on the engagement and "buy-in" of citizens. So Thin Democracy undermines precisely the broad-based commitment our world so desperately needs.

Misaligned with our nature. Thin Democracy can't create healthy societies because it is misaligned with human nature in two ways. Denying our rich complexity, *it fails to tap the best in us and fails to protect us from the worst.*

By "best" I mean several innate needs and capacities I explore in Chapter 2. They include our needs to connect with others, for basic fairness, and for efficacy, as well as the need to feel that our lives matter, which for many people means contributing to something grander than our own survival.

Forcing us to bury these needs, Thin Democracy fuels paralyzing despair and alienation.

Ironically, Thin Democracy doesn't register our really negative potential, either. Let me be clear. I don't mean the capacity of a tiny minority of us; I mean the vast majority. The Holocaust doesn't prove what a crazed dictator and some sadistic guards will do. Actually, it proves the depravity most normal people will express, given the "right" conditions.

To bring home this unhappy truth, British historian Christopher Browning reports that as late as March, 1942, the vast majority—75 to 80 percent—of all victims of the Holocaust were still alive, but "a mere eleven months later" most were dead.[27]

These murders happened, Browning says, because "ordinary" people became killers. He tells, for example, of Reserve Battalion 101—about five hundred men from Hamburg, Germany, many of whom were middle-aged reservists drafted in the fall of 1939.[28] From working and lower middle-classes, these men with no military police experience were sent to Poland on a bloody mission—the total extermination of Jews in Poland's many remote hamlets.[29]

Within four months, they had shot to death, at point-blank range, at least thirty-eight thousand Jews and had another forty-five thousand deported to the concentration camp at Treblinka.[30]

"Though almost all of them—at least initially—were horrified and disgusted," over time, social modeling processes took their toll, as did guilt-induced persuasion by buddies who did the killing, until up to 90 percent of the men in Battalion 101 were involved in the shootings.[31]

I first learned about Battalion 101 from Philip Zimbardo. You might recognize the name. Zimbardo is the professor who organized the infamous "prison experiment" at Stanford in 1971. He put young people who'd "tested normal" into a mock prison setting where they were divided into prisoners and guards, dressed for their roles, and told the experiment would last two weeks.

But on the sixth day, Zimbardo abruptly halted the experiment. He had to. Using some techniques eerily similar to those in Abu Ghraib prison over three decades later, the "guards" had begun brutalizing their "prisoners" causing severe emotional breakdown. Professor Zimbardo has since acknowledged that one reason he stopped the experiment is that his girlfriend told him he himself had begun behaving like a warden—"more concerned," as he put it later, "about the security of 'my prison' than the needs of the young men entrusted to my care..."[32]

In the last one hundred years, humans have killed roughly forty million other humans not in war, as we normally define it, but in massive assaults on civilians, from the fifteen million lost in the Russian Gulag to almost one million in Rwanda. Whether we're talking about a psychologist's carefully designed experiment or the current genocide in Darfur, the inescapable proof is in: Decent people do evil things under the "right conditions."

And what is one condition certain to bring forth brutality? Extreme power imbalances that arise inevitably in a range of social orders. One of these is Thin Democracy.

Failure to bring meaning. Finally, Thin Democracy is dangerously vulnerable because its materialistic premise can't satisfy our higher selves' yearning for transcendent meaning.

Thin Democracy's narrow, insulting assumptions about human nature cannot sustain dedication and sacrifice. Many U.S. soldiers now risk their lives in war, believing they're serving a high calling. But the built-in logic of one-rule economics mocks their idealism. Since 9/11, thousands of American soldiers have made the ultimate sacrifice in Iraq, while executives of U.S. armament corporations have made a killing, doubling their own compensation.[33]

At the same time, Thin Democracy's demeaning materialism and its concentrated wealth help to swell the numbers of excluded people who feel humiliated and angry. Understandably, these feelings open some hearts to extremist, violent ideologies—both religious and secular—that claim high moral ground and offer adherents everlasting glory.

"My grandmother's gone to heaven because she shot the Israelis," explained six-year-old Israa, as she played beneath a photo of seventy-year-old Fatima Najar, who blew herself up in Gaza in 2006. Young men have long seemed most susceptible to violent ideologies, but a sixty-five-year-old in Gaza told the British *Observer*, "I know at least twenty of us [elder women] who want to put on the [suicide bomber's] belt." They've "found a use for themselves," she said.[34]

How deep runs our need to feel useful, a need unmet for so many people in today's world. Ultimately, Thin Democracy can't hold a candle to the fanatics' uplifting, absolutist visions—right or left.

In all, Thin Democracy gives democracy itself a bad name. Its profound shortcomings help to explain why in many countries' initial enthusiasm for it is now waning. In 2000, two-thirds of Latin Americans polled said they were dissatisfied with democracy. Between 2000 and 2005, in ten African countries, polls show citizens' preference for democracy falling—in Tanzania by almost half.[35]

HUMILITY AND HOPE

In "getting a grip" myself, I've tried to shape a way of seeing the world that has explanatory power for me: Our primary obstacle, I lay out here, is that we're stuck in an unworkable mental map that cannot come to grips with local-to-global crises—Thin Democracy.

My diagnosis is hard-nosed about human frailty without writing off our species as incorrigible, for I am reminded almost daily that, as creatures of the mind, we have the unique power to bring to consciousness a failing mental frame—those core assumptions shaping our view of reality—and to remake it with new information and experience.

[E]ach person has the biological power to interrupt
detrimental, derogatory beliefs and generate new ideas.
These new ideas, in turn, can alter the neural circuitry that
governs how we behave and what we believe.

—ANDREW NEWBERG, M.D., AUTHOR, *WHY WE BELIEVE WHAT WE BELIEVE*[36]

We can intentionally evolve more life-serving mental maps. Imagine that!

But to walk this journey presumes a certain kind of humility. With all our fancy forecasting—from ten-day weather reports to the "Fed's" inflation predictions—we can be lulled into believing we can see into the future pretty well. But actually, we can't. History doesn't unfold in neat, even increments. It moves in messy, surprising jolts, and in this unprecedented era, the surprises could even intensify.

And here's the big upside: Recognizing that in this unique moment it is *not possible to know what's possible*…we discover we are free. We're free to throw ourselves into the most thrilling, planetary struggle our species has every known. We can probe deeply, asking together, What might be a richer understanding of democracy—one strong and vital enough to meet today's challenges, and compelling enough to stand up to extremists' claims?

In nine parts, this little book explores this path.

2 NEW EYES

Hope remains only in the most difficult task of all:
to reconsider everything from the ground up,
so as to shape a living society inside a dying society.
—ALBERT CAMUS (1946)[37]

Human beings don't walk into a meaning void. That's not who we are. So if we are to let go of the mental map that is generating Thin Democracy, more is needed than simply acknowledging its frightening pitfalls. We must have at least a glimmer of what can replace it. And that's not easy, for some of the West's most influential opinion shapers carry the presumption of scarcity right down to ideology itself. Referring to corporate capitalism, *New York Times* columnist Thomas Friedman declared, "I don't think there will be an alternative ideology this time around. There are none."[38]

Neither can one suddenly invent out of whole cloth something as profound as a new way of seeing the world. So the great news is that, as democracy reduced to elections plus a one-rule economy is failing, a richer form is taking shape. By its nature, though, it's not as easy to describe as Thin Democracy.

It is, nonetheless, real. Yet because of the way human brains work, we probably won't be able to recognize it unless we believe it's possible. So as much as anything, my goal for this book is to enable us to see possibility: what is happening all around us but still invisible to most of us.

I know the challenge because I was one of the blind ones only a few decades ago as I began asking, what might a workable democracy look like? I figured I'd follow up a few leads on engaged, more participatory forms of problem solving and write a book about what I learned. I expected to turn up a dozen or so examples. In the end, my headache was having to choose among hundreds to write *The Quickening of America*. I still laugh when I recall, on my author's tour, a *U.S. News & World Report* interviewer confessing, "I went to Harvard, and I had never heard about any of what's in your book!"

That book led to several more that have changed my life forever. They've given me a new lens through which I can now see what I like to call Living Democracy—democracy as a way of life, no longer something done *to* us or *for* us but what we ourselves create.

It's new, and it's really old.

Living Democracy furthers a long historical strain expressed throughout our history and in many indigenous practices the world over. Benjamin Franklin, for example, drew on the Iroquois Confederacy's philosophy that, for hundreds of years before one Pilgrim set foot here, had succeeded by practicing inclusive decision making and by valuing diversity.[39] For his part, Thomas Jefferson understood democracy as citizens' everyday participation in public power.

[A]ctive liberty, the principle of participatory self-government, was a primary force shaping the system of government that...[our Constitution] creates.

—SUPREME COURT JUSTICE STEPHEN BREYER[40]

The Living Democracy I see emerging is not merely a formal government set up but is embedded in a wide range of human relationships, so—and here's the vital part—its values apply just as much in economic life or in cultural life as in political life. We don't have to leave our humanity behind when, for instance, we enter the workplace. Put very practically, Living Democracy means infusing the power of citizens' voices and values throughout our public lives and removing the power of money from governance.

Rest assured, Living Democracy isn't a new fixed "ism," blueprint, or utopian end-state. It continually evolves, incorporating new experience as more and more people reject the view that democracy is a *set system* and begin to work with the idea that democracy is a *set of system qualities*, driven by core human values.

The accompanying *Idea 1* contrasts assumptions behind the dominant and failing Thin Democracy with those motivating a richer practice of democracy, one that may become democracy's next historical stage.

IDEA 1: Thin Democracy vs. Living Democracy

THIN DEMOCRACY	LIVING DEMOCRACY
What is it?	
Democracy is a set system: elected government plus a market economy. We may have to keep cleaning it up around the edges, but our democracy is basically complete—it's the culmination of human history.	Living Democracy is a set of system-qualities that shape daily life. Its values of inclusion, fairness, and mutual accountability infuse not only political life but economic and cultural life as well. Living Democracy is always evolving; it's never finished.
How does it work?	
The free market, along with government and corporate executives and experts, determines what happens. Citizens vote, work, and shop. A single rule—highest return to shareholders—drives the market, which does tend to concentrate wealth and power...and then influence the political process. But there's no way other way; tampering with the market would kill its efficiencies and our way of life.	Citizens use their voices and values to shape public choices. They set rules to keep wealth continually circulating and to keep its influence out of politics. They decide what is a market commodity and what is a right of citizenship because it is essential to life. Moving beyond a one-rule economy (highest return to existing wealth), "values boundaries" guide the market, from environmental protections to anti-trust laws; and citizens' conscious shopping choices foster healthy communities
Who gets involved?	
Only officials and celebrities have public lives. Citizens choose them to carry the responsibility.	All citizens have public lives. As buyers, savers, investors, voters, advocates, students, employers, workers, and members of social benefit organizations, our actions create the quality of our communities and the wider world.

What's required for effectiveness?	
Public life is ugly and alienating. No special learning is needed, just thick skins and big egos! (And access to big bucks.)	Democracy is a learned art. As we practice its arts—active listening, creative conflict, negotiation, mediation, mentoring and other relational skills—we reap the joy of effectiveness.
What motivates people to engage?	
Self-defense. Getting involved in public affairs is a necessary hassle to defend our private lives and interests. It is the burden a free people must bear to "earn" our liberties.	We humans know our own well-being depends on healthy communities and that only in public engagement can we fulfill our need to connect with others in common purpose, to make a difference, to express our values and to fully respect ourselves. Engagement is part of the good life.

Okay. As you've glanced at the contrasts in *Idea I*, did Living Democracy strike you as naïve or utopian, even if you didn't want it to? Before exploring more deeply the qualities I see shaping Living Democracy, let me address a core reservation I sense in so many people.

GOODNESS *OF* OR *IN* HUMAN NATURE?

Despite growing evidence to the contrary, a lot of us assume human beings aren't up to the task Living Democracy implies. Most people just want to be left alone, we're told. In fact, the right-wing leader Grover Norquist names his anti-tax movement the Leave Us Alone Coalition. By this logic, Living Democracy *is* naïve, even dangerous, because its emergence would require changing our very nature—at best, a hopeless proposition; at worst, a coercive nightmare.

Behavior proving the skeptics right is, of course, what we see every day in the media. But human beings are a lot more complex than this reductive frame would make us, and, this richness, too, is what we see everyday...*if we open our eyes to it.*

> *So far as I am aware, we [Westerners] are the only society on earth that thinks of itself as having risen from savagery, identified with a ruthless nature. Everyone else believes they are descended from gods.*
>
> —MARSHALL SAHLINS, BIOLOGIST[41]

So the way forward seems clear: We can drop the distracting debate about the goodness *of* human nature and look for the goodness *in* human nature. With this frame, we can get rid of triggers proven to bring out the worst in us, and we can deliberately build on those that bring out the best, our clearly life-affirming needs and capacities: to be cooperative, to be fair, to be effective, and to search for meaning.

First, we're cooperators. Darwin's misconstrued notions about survival competition notwithstanding, it turns out that cooperation explains our evolutionary success just as much. Human beings learned in our early tribal experience that our best chance to thrive is within communities that work for everybody.

Humans are unique among animals in our "pervasive sharing" of food, "especially among unrelated individuals," writes Michael Gurven, a leading authority on transfers among hunter-gatherers living as our early forebears did.[42] Except in times of extreme privation, when some eat, all eat. And the most productive hunters share the most.[43]

Cooperation, which energizes the practices I'm calling Living Democracy, flows in part from hard-wired empathy—increasingly well documented: "Brain imaging studies reveal," writes psychologist Daniel Goleman, "that when we answer the question, 'How are you feeling?' we activate much of the same neural circuitry that lights up when we ask, 'How is she feeling?' The brain acts almost identically when we sense our own feelings and those of another."[44]

Babies cry at the sound of other babies crying, Goleman also notes, but not at a recording of their own cries. And there's certainly no reason to think we humans might be *less* empathetic than Rhesus monkeys, who've been shown in an experiment to forego food (in some cases to starve themselves for up to twelve days) to protect another monkey from electric shock.[45]

Neuroscientists using MRI scans discovered that when human beings cooperate, the same parts of our brains light up that are aroused when we eat chocolate! They note what, of course, even a moment's reflection tells us: We're hardwired to enjoy cooperation.[46]

[Man] is sensible...that his own interest is connected with the prosperity of society, and that the happiness, perhaps the preservation of his existence, depends upon its preservation.

—ADAM SMITH, *THE THEORY OF MORAL SENTIMENTS*, 1790[47]

Second, a sense of fairness lives within most of us, for we have learned that injustice destroys the community on which we're so dependent. Even the supposed godfather of greed, Adam Smith, grasped this truth. Of all the social virtues, Smith wrote more than two centuries ago, we are "in some peculiar manner tied, bound and obliged to the observation of justice."[48] Today researchers are finding even Capuchin monkeys demonstrate a measurable sense of fairness.[49]

Third, we're problem solvers. Thin Democracy's assumptions shrink humans to spectators, shoppers, and whiners. But Living Democracies assume we are also *doers*. How could we possibly have become the dominant species unless we are problem solvers who enjoy seeing the impact of our work?

Our need to "make a dent" in the wider world, as Erich Fromm expressed it, is so great that he revised seventeenth-century René Descartes' thought-focused notion of self. Fromm sums us up this way: "I am, because I effect."[50]

Finally, we're creatures of meaning. Living Democracy replaces the simple materialism of Thin Democracy with the assumption that we human beings want our days to have value beyond ensuring our own survival; and one way we've long met that need is by striving to be good ancestors, enhancing our children's and their children's futures. As we "live democracy," we quench part of our thirst for meaning by contributing to the rescue of our threatened planet and, on the way, enhance qualities deep inside us—empathy, leadership, and courage—this journey brings forth.

This yearning for transcendent meaning runs as deep as any biological urge, certainly. Might it surprise you to learn that roughly the same number, four hundred million, of Google sites turn up whether you search for "sex" or search for "God"?

AN ECOLOGY OF DEMOCRACY: FIVE QUALITIES

Living Democracy, possible because of this richly complex nature of ours, isn't a *set system*. Above I described it instead as a *set of system qualities*. And it's important that we begin to name these qualities, for human beings have a hard time creating what we have no words to describe. Here, then, is my stab at five qualities I see transforming democracy into a lived practice able to solve problems that have seemed insurmountable.

1 dynamic, never finished

Living Democracy is a work in progress to which each new generation applies the lessons of its experience. Between our nation's founding and 2006, our fifty states have ratified over six thousand state constitutional amendments.[51] Its dynamism means Living Democracy isn't limited to redressing singular injustices; it's able to create ever-more inclusive, fairer ways of making decisions. A "learning democracy" might be another apt moniker to describe what is emerging.

> *Democracy is a process, not a static condition:*
> *It can be easily lost, but never is fully won.*
> —JUDGE WILLIAM HASTIE[52]

One recent "sighting" of this dynamism is "participatory budgeting," a newly emerging form of citizen deliberation over key public choices. It began in Brazil where the wealthy have long held a tight grip on how city funds are allotted. To break the grip, in 1990 members of Brazil's Workers' Party—now one of the country's largest—came up with participatory budgeting, a process in which as much as a fifth of a city's budget gets allocated through multi-step, face-to-face neighborhood deliberations.[53]

In the birthplace of citizen budgeting, the southern Brazilian city of Porto Alegre, some one hundred thousand citizens have so far taken part. As a result, the share of resources going to poorer parts of the city and to programs benefiting the poor has grown.

Another dividend? The noticeable decline in corruption under the watchful eyes of so many citizens. Visiting a neighborhood near Porto Alegre in 2003, I admired the big, new community center and heard about a new school and clinic. Asking, "But, how can you afford all this?" I was told by smiling locals that less corruption meant more funds for the community. Plus, the new participatory system means greater government efficiency: In 1988, an administrative dollar in Porto Alegre brought three dollars in services; ten years later it brought seven dollars' worth.[54]

Participatory budgeting has spread to more than three hundred Brazilian cities, and their experience has inspired scores of others around the world to try it, from Durban, South Africa, to Saint-Denis, France.[55] And here at home, in a handful of cities—Portland, Oregon; Seattle, Washington; Birmingham, Alabama;

Dayton, Ohio; and Saint Paul, Minnesota, for example, citizens engage through a range of official channels to guide public spending and inititate community improvements.

Living Democracy's dynamism—its unending evolution—can also be glimpsed in the new, legally binding "community benefit agreements" you'll read about in the following chapter.

2   values guided, not dogma driven

Just mentioning the word "values" unnerves many Americans; they believe we're hopelessly divided, so best not to go there. In truth, we're hope*fully* united on some essential policies reflecting deeply shared values. Almost nine in ten of us favor raising the federal minimum wage. Almost eight in ten say we should do whatever it takes to protect the environment. And roughly two in three agree our government should guarantee health care for all, even if it means higher taxes.[56]

These specifics reflect more general values infusing the dynamism of effective democracy: fairness, inclusion, and mutual accountability. By "mutual accountability," I mean simply all sides shouldering responsibility. Pointing fingers at those up there—the president, the CEO—isn't enough. Bemoaning our victimhood isn't enough.

Jack Shipley, a sixty-six-year-old, part-time rancher near Grants Pass, Oregon, helped teach me this lesson. Jack is a leader in the Applegate Partnership, entrusted by the state with watershed protection planning for an eight-hundred-square-mile chunk of southern Oregon.

"The environmentalists criticize us for talking to loggers," Jack told me a few years ago. "But how can we find solutions if we don't include all people who are part of the problem?" he asks. So members of Jack's group, the Applegate Partnership, began wearing a signature button around town: one word with the familiar "no" slash through it. The word is "They."

If there is no "they" to blame, we realize all sides need to act. And did, arriving at a plan all could accept.

Another example of "mutual accountability" in action that brings to life the values of fairness and inclusion began in south Texas in 1990. Jolted by the closing of a Levi Strauss plant that left one thousand people jobless, two San Antonio church-based groups began searching for ways to ease the plight of the unemployed and of poor workers.

Communities Organized for Public Service (COPS)—which reaches fifty thousand families through twenty-seven parishes—and its sister organization, Metro Alliance, were upset. They saw new, well-paying jobs were being created, but San Antonio's many low-skill job seekers, many of them Hispanic, weren't filling them. Yes, the citizen groups could easily have jumped on the big companies, calling them racist for not hiring locals. Instead, they decided to be problem solvers: They identified the real stumbling block as the lack of effective job training.

Then the two organizations' members—homemakers, bus drivers, ministers—formed a committee to come up with a solution themselves. The fruit of their labor is QUEST—Quality Employment Through Skills Training—now boasting almost two thousand graduates who are prepared not just for any job but for skilled, well-paying ones. Eighteen months after graduating, almost 80 percent of QUEST participants have jobs with an average hourly wage several times higher than in the minimum wage jobs many had held.[57] Four other cities have replicated QUEST's model and together have trained fifty-five hundred people.

Driven by widely shared values not fixed dogma, Living Democracy evolves as citizens bring those values to public engagement.

3   learned, not automatic

Humans are innately social beings, it's true, but that doesn't mean we're necessarily born knowing how to "do democracy" effectively. So more and more people worldwide are coming to understand democracy not as something we simply inherit and defend but as a learned art. Democratic skills, they are saying, can and must be deliberately taught—and practiced—just as are reading or cooking or dribbling a basketball.

Of course, if we're not good at any these things, they're not much fun. Running after tennis balls for hours, I've learned, gets pretty tedious. But as we gain skills, including those of "doing democracy," our lives become ever more rewarding.

Young people are among those catching on and leading the way.

In the spring of 2007 at the University of California Santa Cruz, I met with students who had created their own strikingly successful course, the Education for Sustainable Living Program. Now in its fourth year, the course has spread to six California campuses. Three hundred eager students are enrolled in Santa Cruz. "We could never have gotten this course off the ground," initiator Aurora Winslade, told me, "if the eight students who started it hadn't studied communication skills together and committed ourselves to use them with each other."

Chapter 5 suggests that schools, businesses, community institutions, and elected bodies are effectively learning democratic arts such as *active listening*, addressing conflict through *negotiation* and *mediation*, as well as *mentoring* and *reflecting on experience*.

4 power-creating, not controlling

So much political talk obsesses over who's got power and who's losing it—as if there were only so much to go around. (One more instance of the scarcity presumption?) Yet, taken to its Latin root, *posse*, power means "to be able," simply our capacity to act. So maybe we should be talking less about power's division and more about its creation—what's really needed to solve our problems.

Living Democracy practices create more power by enabling more people to act on their values and interests. In other words, Living Democracy widens the circle of problem solvers. It expands problem-solving power because it taps into the experience and insight of people closest to the problem. It thrives on the creativity engendered when diverse perspectives meet and the commitment to action that people willingly make when they "own" and are a valued part of the plan.

In a successful struggle to decentralize school decision making in Hammond, Indiana, participant Patrick O'Rourke captured this notion of expanding power, noting that the new set up "broadens the base of decision making in a way that empowers everyone… [B]uilding administrators don't lose out if teachers are more creative…they win. Everyone wins."[58]

Chapter 4, *Power Invisible*, explores the notion of generative, relational power.

5 everywhere, not isolated

Finally, and perhaps best of all, Living Democracy's values "work" throughout the many dimensions of our lives, not just the political. So it's possible to align our inner selves. Citizens don't have to chop ourselves in pieces and leave some of the best of us at home as we venture into our public lives.

What a boon to sanity.

Notice that I'm using public life to refer not just to what officials have but to all the roles we play—including voter, buyer, employer, investor, saver, worker, and volunteer, as *Idea 2* suggests. Living Democracy's values apply from politics and economics to education, policing, the media, and more, as the next chapter sketches. This is what I mean by "everywhere."

But trickiest to grasp is democracy emerging in economic life, so I'll dwell here a moment.

The ecological worldview in which Living Democracy is emerging enables us to see ourselves not as isolated atoms but as

IDEA 2: We All Have Public Lives

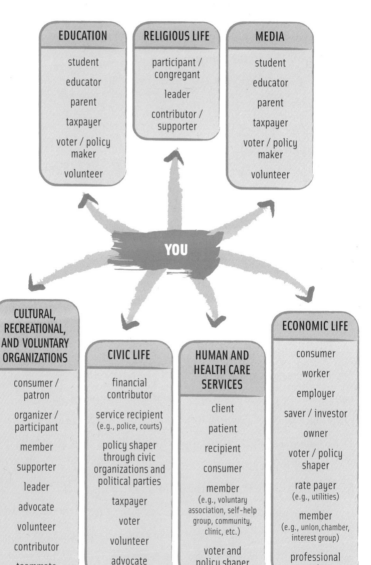

EDUCATION
- student
- educator
- parent
- taxpayer
- voter / policy maker
- volunteer

RELIGIOUS LIFE
- participant / congregant
- leader
- contributor / supporter

MEDIA
- student
- educator
- parent
- taxpayer
- voter / policy maker
- volunteer

YOU

CULTURAL, RECREATIONAL, AND VOLUNTARY ORGANIZATIONS
- consumer / patron
- organizer / participant
- member
- supporter
- leader
- advocate
- volunteer
- contributor
- teammate

CIVIC LIFE
- financial contributor
- service recipient (e.g., police, courts)
- policy shaper through civic organizations and political parties
- taxpayer
- voter
- volunteer
- advocate

HUMAN AND HEALTH CARE SERVICES
- client
- patient
- recipient
- consumer
- member (e.g., voluntary association, self-help group, community, clinic, etc.)
- voter and policy shaper

ECONOMIC LIFE
- consumer
- worker
- employer
- saver / investor
- owner
- voter / policy shaper
- rate payer (e.g., utilities)
- member (e.g., union, chamber, interest group)
- professional associates

nodes in networks of relationships. Corporations then become just one channel we create to organize relationship networks. This means that corporations are *not independent of us or unchangeable monoliths*. A lot changes: We wake up to our own power, the multitude of ways in which we already *do* shape corporations and can redirect them to life-serving ends.

With this view of economic life, businesses respond to market cues, yes, but with accountability-boundaries that citizens set, from tax and trade rules to environmental and buyer-safety protections. We recognize both the formal channels—through governments— and informal influences—including our own daily choices and organized advocacy—we can use to keep the market fair and life-promoting. As Lizzie Maggie tried to alert us, we citizens have to take the rule-setting function of economic life seriously, or our society ends up like Monopoly at the end of the evening…the fun's over for everybody because one player gets all the property.

Once seeing the economy embedded in a culture of democracy, buyers also use the power of marketplace choices to send ripples demanding healthy and fair practices to producers, as in the growing Fair Trade movement I pick up in the next chapter.

A PREMISE OF PLENTY, A SPIRAL OF HOPE

In contrast to the premise of lack in the opening *Spiral of Powerlessness*, these five qualities generate a spiral of human growth and satisfaction I've striven to capture in the *Spiral of Empowerment* you'll find inside the back cover.

Its premise is plenty—that as we come to appreciate and enjoy nature's laws, learning to live within a self-renewing ecological home, we discover there's more than enough for all to live well.

This realization I first experienced as a lightning bolt, when in my twenties I learned that there was more than enough food in the world to make us all chubby...and there still is, even considering staggering built-in waste.

I learned that we create the scarcity we fear.

Worldwide, for example, more than a third of all grain and 90 percent of soy gets fed to livestock.[59] Future generations may well scratch their heads: You mean, in the early twenty-first century their feedlot system put 16 pounds of grain and soy into cattle to produce only *one* pound of beef on their plates? You mean that with the amount of water they used for that one pound of beef they could bathe for a year?

I learned that this irrationality took off, even though inefficient and harmful to health, because one-rule economics leaves millions of people too poor to buy food and keeps grain so cheap that it's profitable to feed vast amounts to animals.

Beyond food, the U.S. economy remains "astoundingly" wasteful, conclude the authors of *Natural Capitalism*, as "only 6 percent of its vast flows of materials actually end up in products."[60]

Imagine, then, the potential plenty, not to mention health benefits, as we shift toward equity and efficiency.

Similar plenty appears once we drop the scarcity lens surrounding energy. Our sun, wind, waves, water, and biomass offer us a "daily dose of energy" 15,000 times greater than in all the planet-harming fossil and nuclear power we now use, says German energy expert Hermann Scheer. Just one-fifth of the energy in wind alone would, if converted to electricity, meet the whole world's energy demands, reports a Stanford-NASA study.[61]

An awareness of plenty itself undermines a focus on raw, self-centered competition, leaving us able to refocus not on the goodness *of* human nature, which seems to deny human complexity, but on the undeniable goodness *in* human nature, including the deep positive needs and capacities just mentioned.

From there, the *Spiral of Empowerment* quickens. We gain confidence that we can learn to make sound decisions together about the rules that further healthy communities. Then, as we begin to succeed and ease the horrific oppression and conflict that now rob us of life, we reinforce positive expectations about our species. The destructive mental map loosens its hold. And as these capacities and needs—for fairness, connection, efficacy, and meaning—find avenues for expression, they redound, generating even more creative decision making and outcomes.

So "getting a grip" doesn't have to mean a sober struggle. From this more complete view of our own nature and of what nature offers, could it instead become an exhilarating adventure?

3 WHAT DEMOCRACY FEELS LIKE

'So this is what democracy must feel like.' I bet I've have heard
this twenty different times in completely different settings—
it doesn't feel foreign when people experience it, but
democracy is a need we don't always know we have.

—MARTHA MCCOY

Martha leads the Study Circles Resource Center, a Connecticut group that's helped tens of thousands of Americans discover a need—*experiencing* democracy—that's so seldom met many of us have forgotten we have it.

Her work tells us a lot about what happens when people remember. In 1999, her center began working in Kansas City with a diverse citizen coalition distressed that high school test scores were sinking and half the students were dropping out. This educational breakdown, they realized, was linked to life in neighborhoods where people felt unsafe, disconnected, and powerless. And they wanted to *do* something.

So residents from all walks of life—in the end, over thirteen hundred—began meeting in study circles, creating trust and generating solutions to augment a school reform process already underway. Over just eight years, graduation rates rose to 70 percent. Spanish-speaking parents started and now run a "homework help line." Public housing residents created a tenants' association and youth sports camp and are helping to rid a neighborhood of ten drug houses. In addition, over one hundred young people, including some school-leavers, worked together to clean up the downtown.

Martha and these gutsy Kansans are part of an emergent ecology of democracy in which Americans are discovering what Living Democracy looks, tastes, and sounds like. It's no longer a distant, fixed structure. Democracy "becomes us," they are finding, in both meanings of the phrase. Their actions and parallel ones around the planet are helping to shift our focus from democracy as a thing we "have"—elections, parties, a market—to democracy as intricate relationships of mutuality that we create daily.

To give you a sense of this new way of seeing (and being) democracy, here are just nine of its many dimensions, along with hints of how they are already changing lives.

NINE DIMENSIONS: SOME GLIMPSES

1 Citizens are reclaiming their political power from the grip of concentrated wealth.

New Yorkers, angry that both major parties answer more to corporate interests than to them, have broken the two-party lockdown. In only nine years, working people in New York State have created their own Working Families Party. With "cross-endorsement" voting, which allows a party to use its ballot line for its own or another party's candidate, Working Families got a foothold. It's already helped pass key reforms, including a two-dollar hourly hike in the state minimum wage.

In only a decade, grassroots-led reforms for voluntary public financing, called Clean Elections, have significantly purged private wealth from elections in Maine and Arizona. (A similar Connecticut law will take effect in 2008.) In Arizona, nine of eleven state offices are now held by those who "ran clean"—i.e., qualified for public financing by taking no private money beyond the initial few dollars from the minimum number of citizens needed to get on the ballot.

So citizens are starting to trust again. Voter turnout in Arizona has jumped over a quarter in presidential elections since 1998.[62] People with modest incomes, like teachers, can seek office—and win.

Other states have made certain races "clean," and a movement to take Clean Elections national is gaining steam. It asks us to weigh the price of *not* acting: Each American household is now paying out $1,600 yearly in tax breaks, subsidies, and other welfare for corporations and wealthy special interests—the tip of the iceberg of the true cost of private power over the public purse.[63] Compare it to the cost of eliminating big-donor influence using a Federal Clean Elections approach: Just $6 annually for each of us would cover the costs of all campaigns for national office—thus, the new movement's Website: just6dollars.org.

An obvious bargain.

2   Citizens are striving to make government their tool: a fair-standard
    setter, a public convener and more—so government isn't burdened by
    the job of damage control.

In Thin Democracy dogma, Big Government is the bugaboo: It steals
our money and our privacy. "Government is not the solution to our
problem; government is the problem," Ronald Reagan warned us in
his first inaugural address. Citizens are made to fear that going for
what they desire and know is right, like ending poverty and rescuing
the environment, would unleash the big, bad state.

So they pull back.

The maddening irony is that those who scare us with fear of
Big Brother government are too often the same people turning
governing over to private interests...and thus *making* it scary.

But Living Democracy depends on seeing through this mind-
twist. It depends on citizens shaping and trusting government as
their tool. And that starts with exposing the misleading big-versus-
small government frame and recognizing that what really matters
is whether government is accountable to citizens.

*Government's job is to set high standards, let the market
reach them and then raise the standards more.*

—THOMAS L. FRIEDMAN, *THE NEW YORK TIMES*[64]

Accountable government, setting fair standards and rules, actually
reduces the need for "big" government to clean up after the damage
is done. From this frame, we see the cost of government action to

end poverty or to rescue our environment with new eyes. *The real cost is our government's not acting.*

- Since 2000, poverty has grown by almost one million each year, so today thirty-seven million Americans live in poverty, many more than the entire Canadian population.[65] Set aside, if you can, the incalculable human suffering of poverty and the loss to society of human gifts that poverty leaves undeveloped, and consider some of what we can tally up: So many American children, almost one in five, grow up poor that the annual costs to our society from poverty—just counting crime (We spend enough on incarceration to buy a Harvard education for each of the two million, mostly poor, people locked up.[66]), lost economic output, and higher health expenditures—total almost $500 billion.[67]

  That's more than our entire defense budget!

- Similarly, enforcing environmental protection standards is a steal compared to the mega-billions needed to deal with the messes once made. "Superfund" clean-ups of toxic sites have already cost taxpayers tens of billions of dollars since they began in 1980. And because the government has abandoned the polluter-pays principle, over the next thirty years the United States may have to spend up to $250 billion more on as many as three hundred fifty thousand such sites, reports the Environmental Protection Agency.[68] (One in four of us still lives within four miles of these toxic sites.)

Only accountable government can prevent democracy-and-people-killing poverty and pollution. And it's not rocket science; we know how. Remember the 1960s War on Poverty—naysayers' proof of government ineptitude? Actually, Americans cut the poverty rate in half during that decade.[69]

Doing what it takes to uproot poverty—enforcing anti-monopoly laws, protecting employees' right to organize, maintaining a federal minimum wage that's really a living wage, creating job opportunities, assuring universal health care, guaranteeing quality day care for all children—none of this requires big government.

Neither would it enlarge government to restore tax rates aligned with the fairness principle of ability to pay. In at least one recent year, eighty-two top U.S. corporations paid *zero* taxes.[70] And since 1970, average tax rates on the wealthiest one-tenth of one percent of Americans have been cut in half, and tax rates on dividends and capital gains, most relevant to the wealthy, are now lower than the rate on earned income of most middle-class families.[71]

The subjects of every state ought to contribute towards the support of the government, as nearly as possible, in proportion to their relative abilities...

—ADAM SMITH, *THE WEALTH OF NATIONS*, 1776[72]

Moreover, rescuing the environment could start with simply requiring the government to *stop*—stop handing out rewards for destruction. No big price tag there, just the guts to say no to fossil fuel lobbies. An estimated $700 billion worldwide in subsidies now encourage environmentally devastating practices such as over-pumping groundwater, clear-cutting forests, and burning fossil fuel.[73]

My aim here is simply to underscore that we *can* free ourselves from the fear-mongering and follow our hearts and our common sense. Consider this finding: A 2007 in-depth examination of poverty and its cures concludes that it would take only $90 billion a year for ten years to cut U.S. poverty in half. Simply retracting the Bush administration's tax cuts to households earning over $200,000 would more than cover this life-saving turnaround.[74]

As to what citizens are already doing to make government their accountable tool, some are successfully enacting new rules that reset the economic logic now ensuring ecological devastation.

- One is the "producer-responsibility" or "take-back" law I take up in Chapter 9. It requires manufacturers to shoulder responsibility for recovery and reuse of what they put into the world. It's already working in twenty-nine countries, as well as in Maine and Washington State.[75]
- Another commonsense solution to global heating that doesn't enlarge government is "tax shifting." Europeans are beginning to tax "bads," not "goods," to encourage environmental citizenship. Sweden, for example, has lifted on average $1,100 from each household's income tax and shifted it mainly to vehicles and fuel.[76]

In addition to acting as fair-standard setter, government in democracies answerable to citizens can also serve as our efficient financial agent. But how easy it is to get confused here, too. We're told that Social Security, Medicare, and Medicaid are three *entitlement* programs eating up almost half the federal budget. And we think: Egads, big government is killing us.

Entitlement? Of course we're entitled; we paid. But "big government?" I don't think so.

In two of these programs, government collects and dispenses our money, allowing us to support each succeeding generation of retiring elders—without which about 40 percent would now be living in poverty. But here's the little-appreciated fact: Social Security's administrative costs amount to less than 1 percent of benefits. That's a tiny fraction of what privately managed investment accounts charge.[77] And for Medicare, administrative costs run about 2 percent, compared to nearly 12 percent for HMOs.[78] This is what I mean by government as citizens' "efficient agent." Let's not let the need now to fix Social Security—because Reagan, then others, raided its assets to cover tax cuts for the wealthy and more—blind us to its virtues.

Another, most basic, standard-setting task of citizens in Living Democracy is distinguishing between what should and should not be allocated by the market—what is a right of all people because it is essential to life.

- Historically in the U.S. and elsewhere, K-12 education has been a right.
- Most people in industrial societies have also removed health care from the market, saving themselves vast sums while

achieving superior health outcomes. The French, for example, enjoy life expectancy two years longer than we do while spending roughly half as much on health care per person.[79]

- For many, a decent federal minimum wage should also be in the "rights" column, and it sure doesn't seem to slow down an economy: Ireland enjoys a minimum wage almost double ours but surpasses the Unites States in per capita GDP.[80] (Note: If our minimum hourly wage had kept up with CEO compensation, it would now be $22.61!)

Now recognizing the threats of global heating and world poverty, more and more people realize that rescuing our planet—and even having a functioning market—depends on citizens reclaiming government from private interests. We can leave behind any knee-jerk contempt for government and learn from our compatriots in Maine and Arizona, just mentioned, how to wrest government from money's influence so that it can become one essential, powerful tool for creating the world we want.

Finally, a story.

It captures powerfully for me the effectiveness, not costliness, of government in its role as public convener and fair-standard setter, and it comes from Brazil.

In 1993, that country's fourth largest city, Belo Horizonte, reframed access to healthy food as a human right. That mind shift set off enormous ripples. A new city food security agency convened business, civic, union, religious, university, and other leaders who came up with dozens of civic partnerships enabling poor people to get healthy food.

Their outside-the-box innovations include fair-price produce stands on city land, supplied by forty local farmers; open-air restaurants serving twelve thousand subsidized meals daily; and city-sponsored radio broadcasts leading shoppers to the lowest priced essentials. Their ingenuity led to a Green Basket program that links hospitals, restaurants, and other big buyers directly to local, small, organic growers and spurred dozens of community gardens, as well as forty school gardens, to become "live labs" for teaching science and environmental studies.[81]

"We're showing that the state doesn't have to provide everything; it can facilitate. It can create channels for people to find solutions themselves," explained Adriana Aranha, first head of the agency launching the city's hunger-fighting and now a leader in Brazil's national "Zero Hunger" campaign.

The city-coordinated innovations helped reduce the infant death rate, the best measure of hunger, 56 percent in just a decade.

And the cost? *One* percent of the municipal budget.[82]

3 Investors, savers, and purchasers are infusing democratic values into their everyday economic choices.

Living Democracy's values including fairness and mutual accountability are showing up in an invest-with-social-purpose movement that has swollen fifty-three-fold to $2 trillion in two decades. Stock purchasers are realizing they can exert positive power by deliberately choosing companies behaving in ways more aligned with their values and by using their stock ownership to speak out on company policy.

Investor pressure on corporations has been credited with impacts ranging from eliminating discrimination based on sexual orientation at the credit company MBNA to eliminating mercury-containing thermometers sold by J.C. Penney's.[83] Recently, a group of McDonald's shareholders backed Florida's farm workers' demands on that company. The SEC supported them as well, and McDonald's gave in.

And as governments beholden to private interests fail to protect labor rights—with the two nations having the biggest economies, the United States and China, unwilling to ratify basic international labor conventions—purchasers and producers are stepping up. They've partnered to create a Fair Trade economy. In it, a certifying body insures that producers receive a fair price and use environmentally sustainable practices. Fair Trade producer cooperatives also receive a premium to use for such community benefits as a new school.

The certifier attaches a label to Fair Trade products so purchasers determined to end poverty can find them. Already, Fair Trade has lifted over a million coffee-producing families out of destitution. The movement now embraces twenty products and is found in fifty countries. In the United States, more than thirty thousand retail locations carry Fair Trade Certified products, including Target, CostPlus, Starbucks, and Costco.

In the U.K., half the population recognizes the Fair Trade label.[84] True, most Americans have yet to hear of the Fair Trade movement, but in 2005 French President Jacques Chirac declared its founder, priest Frans Van der Hoff, a Knight of the French Legion of Honor, to focus the French on the transforming potential of what Van der Hoff had begun just over two decades ago.

4   Citizens are setting values boundaries within which corporations function.

In one sense, Living Democracy means returning corporations to the role envisioned by our founders: they are instruments to serve society's well being.

In this light, muscular campaigns by citizens to redirect the behavior of corporate giants are not a separate species of "activism" but a key part of democracy-building. For example, in 1997, Rainforest Action Network, then with a staff of only twenty-five and a handful of conscientious shareholders, ratcheted up its challenge to Home Depot for using wood from ancient, largely untouched forests.

Some probably scoffed. Who would have bet that their ingenious efforts (including using Home Depot's own store intercoms to enlighten shoppers) would within two years convince the company to halt its use of old-growth wood, triggering a cascade among other big wood-suppliers wanting to avoid bad publicity?

And who could have imagined that in 2003, even as Big Tobacco kicked and screamed, two hundred citizens' groups, the World Health Organization, and leaders from forty-six African countries could succeed in birthing the world's first public health treaty: the Global Tobacco Treaty? It bars tobacco corporations from advertising or interfering with public policymaking. One hundred forty-seven nations—but not the United States—have ratified it.[85] The magnitude of their triumph hit me when I learned that, if current trends hold, tobacco will kill one billion people by century's end.[86]

Communities are also creating new legal tools that set values boundaries within which corporations function.

In Los Angeles in 2001, the Staples Center sought a $70 million downtown expansion, and twenty-five citizens' groups pulled enough weight to win the nation's first big "community benefits agreement"—not a bunch of feel-good promises but legally binding accords with businesses and local governments guaranteeing that living-wage jobs, affordable housing, and environmental protections are part of the expansion.

After that sweet 2001 victory, one citizen group set its sights higher: a piece of the $11 billion expansion of the Los Angeles International Airport, around which are "the most densely populated neighborhoods of any airport in the country and among the poorest in L.A.," Madeline Janis-Aparicio told me. She heads the Los Angeles Alliance for a New Economy, a hybrid research-communications-organizing outfit founded in 1993.

"The airport had increasingly horrible consequences for people living there—the worst rates of asthma, and noise so fierce you can't hear yourself speak. So some schools have no windows; they're like fortresses—horrendous.

"When we started, fatalism—'There's nothing we can do'—had set in. It was the 'coalition of the defeated,'" Madeline said. "But groups came together—labor, teachers, parents, neighborhood associations—and we spent a year building trust. People began to feel they could dream, and over ten months, we negotiated among ourselves exactly which seventy priorities we'd ask for. We trained people to be negotiators.

"And we won"—half a billion dollars in community benefits funds.

"It even means moving a whole school," said Madeline, "and millions for job training. It means every single employer that even touches the airport has to go to the community first to fill jobs." The agreement also includes money to reduce airport noise, emissions, and traffic, and it assures ongoing monitoring of the airport's health impact on residents.

"All this came out of the community, some of it from people who'd never taken on anything beyond demanding a stoplight, if that," Madeline told me excitedly. Citizens trained to be spokespeople, to organize community meetings, and to hold effective press conferences. They found their voices to stand up for their community.

At least a dozen such Community Benefit Agreements are in the works. In New York, Milwaukee, and San Diego, they have already been achieved, Madeline said, and she's convinced they will "reshape the nature of land use and economic development."

Before moving on to the next dimension of Living Democracy, let me break with the positive for a critical point: This task—citizens setting the values boundaries within which corporations function—has been made significantly harder by an invisible-to-the-general-public shift over the last one hundred fifty years. Remember that at the corporation's birth in the early 1800s, there was no confusion about who was in charge: it was chartered by local governments to meet particular needs such as building a road or bridge. But beginning in the mid-

1800s, with the rise of the influence of the Robber Barons, corporations began acquiring for themselves Supreme-Court-recognized rights—due process, free speech, equal protection, and more—that enable them to defy the public's will: for example, to block enforceable standards they don't like or to influence the outcome of elections.

> ...constitutional ordinances earned on the field of battle as charters of human liberty, have been turned into the shield of incorporated monopoly.
> —SEYMOUR D. THOMPSON, ADDRESS TO KANSAS BAR ASSOCIATION, 1892[87]

The oxymoron "corporate personhood" evolved to describe this democracy-defeating ascendance of private power.

In response, a movement of diverse citizens—including Republicans, Democrats, Libertarians, and Progressives—is fighting to reverse the granting of constitutional protections to these non-human entities. In late 2006, the township of East Brunswick, Pennsylvania, became the eighth local government to abolish the accumulated personhood "rights" and legal privileges claimed by corporations and the fourth to legally recognize the rights of nature, as well.[88]

Recently in St. Thomas Township, Pennsylvania, population fifty-six hundred, a corporate challenge to democracy occurred that should send chills down the spines of all Americans. A corporation threatened to sue the town if an elected official weighed in on its request to create a limestone quarry near a school there.

Why? The company claimed that because the official had campaigned on a platform opposing the quarry, its *constitutional* right to due process would be violated if the official spoke. It worked: the official shut up. Surely if corporations can successfully claim constitutional rights to muzzle public servants elected to represent our views, we will have lost democracy itself. A group of St. Thomas citizens are themselves now suing the state over this violation.[89]

But let's step back.

At our founding, "we the people" meant we *real* people, of course. Corporations are not mentioned in our constitution; they came on the scene to further "we the people's" welfare. As agents to serve humanity, corporations themselves legitimately have no *inherent* rights; only people do.

Corporations do have numerous legal protections that we the people grant them and can revoke—including, for example, a corporation's limited legal liability, bankruptcy protection, virtual immortality (since their charters are rarely revoked), and a whole legal structure to protect their contracts.

These legal privileges (not to mention huge public subsidies), added to their claim of inherent constitutional rights and their vastly superior resources relative to real people, mean corporations inevitably tilt to their benefit any political playing field of real people.

But democracy requires a level playing field. And that's what citizens of Humboldt County, California, for example, are shooting for. There, Wal-Mart and the logging giant Maxxam had in recent years each spent hundreds of thousands of dollars to influence votes to serve their interests. So in mid-2006, a citizens' initiative banned from elections the use of money from non-locally owned corporations and other entities. [90]

5   At the same time even some mega-corporations are redefining the bottom-line to align profit with the prospering of the planet.

Increasing numbers of corporations are realizing that, actually, they're not required by their legal charters to seek only narrow, immediate gains for shareholders and CEOs, while leaving waste and destruction for the rest of us to clean up. Some are acknowledging mounting evidence that responsible businesses bring higher returns on average than do their less ethical competitors.[91] The one hundred ninety companies of the World Business Council for Sustainable Development, for example, have outperformed their respective stock exchanges by 15 to 25 percent over the last three years.[92]

Investor and buyer pressure is at play here, but so are some real human beings at the helm.

Consider the difference those human beings can make: GE, whose former head Jack Welch once scoffed at climate-change science and called mandated toxics clean-up unconstitutional, is now lead by Jeffrey Immelt who sees sustainable energy as a "business imperative." The company has quadrupled its wind energy revenues since it acquired the business in 2002 and says it will double its clean energy investments by 2010. GE has also caught on that businesses need a level playing field to act on this good-business/

good-planet sense that only government rules ensure, so GE is one of dozens of companies bucking the Bush administration and advocating federally set carbon emissions restrictions.

Americans' growing appetite for healthy food and sound corporate values has enabled Whole Foods Market to mushroom from founder John Mackey's 1980 Austin storefront to 195 stores, swallowing smaller competitors. Its "whole foods, whole people, whole planet" mission plays out in the company's emphasis on organic foods, support for local farmers, use of renewable energy, and its "Animal Compassionate Standards." Company values include giving workers a voice: "I could have clerked anywhere," a checkout person in Austin told me in late 2006, "but here, we have a real voice. It's the team that decides who gets hired." And, while most CEO pay climbs skyward, Mackey as of 2007 receives one dollar annually.

Yet Mackey resists unions that would allow workers an independent voice—in 2003 describing unions as "highly unethical."[93] And, in 2007 the Federal Trade Commission sued to stop what it sees as Mackey's anti-competitive attempt to buy his last big rival, Wild Oats, and questioned his tactics.

So, here's the question for Living Democracy:

Can we learn to hold two seemingly contrary truths at once? Can we encourage desperately needed positive corporate actions and, without blinking, also recognize that, no matter how conscientious the economic giants become, their concentrated power and ability to buy political influence contradict democracy?

6   Citizens are generating "local living economies" by standing up for hometown businesses as they disperse economic power, reduce energy waste, and build community bonds.

"Buy Local or Bye-Bye Local." "Be a Local Lover." These two bumper stickers you might spot these days in Bellingham, Washington, a city of sixty-seven thousand. And on storefronts, T-shirts, flyers, and newspaper pages in this bayside city, you'll also see the slogan, "Think Local, Buy Local, Be Local." All are signs of Sustainable Connections, a coalition of locally owned businesses that, in 2003, launched a "local first" campaign.

"'Are you locally owned?' Since the campaign started, more and more businesses are hearing the question," Michelle Long, executive director of Sustainable Connections, told me.

"Before, the question never came up."

Now, more than five hundred participating independent businesses display a poster and a "buy local" decal in their windows. They give special thank-you cards to loyal customers and offer customers coupon books with discounts at member stores.

To kick off the campaign, Sustainable Connections welcomed citizens to compete to collect the most receipts from local businesses in one month. The grand prize? A month of free meals at locally owned restaurants.

A dollar spent in a locally owned business can generate three times more local economic activity than a dollar paid to a corporate chain.[94] Not to mention the community building that happens when we shop from proprietors we know and the enormous environmental benefit of shortening supply chains. Fifty other cities also participate in the growing Business Alliance for Local Living Economies

This may seem dreamy if all we hear about is corporate globalization, but almost 60 percent of our GDP still comes from locally owned outfits largely selling locally, says *Small-Mart Revolution* author Michael Shuman.

7   Businesses that close the gap between owners and workers are growing fast, proving that markets can work splendidly without control by outside capital.

Cooperatives are democratic businesses in which the owners are also the business's workers or users of its services. In all their varieties—from finance to housing, farming, manufacturing and more—equitable sharing of responsibilities and benefits is a key value. Co-op membership has more than doubled in the last thirty years, now providing one hundred million jobs worldwide. That's one-fifth *more* than multinational corporations offer, says the Geneva-based International Co-operative Alliance.

Around the world, roughly eight hundred million people are now co-op members—outnumbering the number who own shares in publicly traded companies.[95] Three of the top four countries ranked by the World Economic Forum as having the world's most competitive economies are also among the top four in share of sales contributed by co-ops: Finland, Switzerland, and Sweden.[96]

Are you surprised? I certainly was. But then again, when was the last time you saw a "co-op" section in your newspaper's "business pages"?

- In Italy's Emilia Romagna region, a network of five thousand diverse cooperatives generate over 30 percent of economic output, and the region is one of the wealthiest in Europe.
- In Colombia, the Saludcoop health care co-op, the nation's second largest employer, provides services to a quarter of the population.
- In Kuwait, 80 percent of all retail sales are rung up by the Union of Consumer Co-operative Societies.
- In India, a network of over one hundred thousand village dairy cooperatives, owned by nearly eleven million members, are largely responsible for India's becoming the world's biggest milk producer.[97]

Closer to home is Organic Valley, an organic dairy cooperative formed in the late 1980s by a handful of Wisconsin dairy farmers distressed that their neighbors' farms were folding while profits were going everywhere but to farmers. I admit I would never have predicted that in less than two decades their determination would birth a multi-million dollar company owned by almost a thousand family farmers in twenty-five states. Organic Valley still lives by its democratic values, with profits returning to farmers and rural communities.

8   In thousands of schools and universities, students are learning democracy by doing it.

Students are moving from "community service" in which adults are in charge to "apprentice citizenship" in which young people take ownership in hands-on learning. Most important, they experience their own power to make real, lasting improvements in their communities. From environmental restoration to improving their school food service, grade schoolers in forty school districts in New England are learning by becoming community problem solvers as part of a movement led by Maine's KIDS Consortium.

"I realized I was saving lives. Now that's the shocking part," a Maine sixth grader told me after taking leadership in a public safety campaign through KIDS.

Young people experiencing power as problem-solvers enhances academic achievement. In southern Ohio, as public school students in Federal Hocking High gained power—including equal voice with teachers in hiring faculty—the percentage going on to college climbed in a decade from 20 to 70 percent.

In local food movements, students in dozens of colleges—from Santa Cruz to Cornell—are leading the charge, linking local, sustainable, democratic food and farming to their school's food services. And in one hundred sixty-four U.S. universities, students are learning to hold administrators accountable for buying school products only from companies using fair-labor practices.[98]

9   In law enforcement, community-based policing and restorative-
    justice approaches are reducing crime and healing communities.

In forty-seven states, volunteer citizen boards help decide the
appropriate treatment for nonviolent transgressors, repairing harm
done and guiding violators' reintegration into the community,
with huge public savings.[99]

Community policing—police and citizens partnering to reduce
crime—was introduced in the 1980s but really took off during the
Clinton administration. It is as much about keeping problems from
entering the criminal justice doorway as it is about nabbing criminals. In
Cincinnati, Ohio, almost one thousand city-trained volunteers, called
Citizens on Patrol, cover twenty-four neighborhoods in the city.[100]

Thus, from political life to economic life to education, expectations of ourselves and others are changing, and the five qualities
of Living Democracy noted in the previous chapter are showing
up. For hundreds more stories in this vein—not random acts of
sanity but innovations deepening and enlivening the very meaning of democracy—please see reading recommendations at the
end of the book.

WHY NOW? FOUR REVOLUTIONS

Who could say with any certainty why such dramatic changes are
underway? But here is my best hunch. Four revolutions are putting wind in the sails of Living Democracy:

1 A communications-knowledge revolution.

Instantaneous global communication is allowing us to experience ourselves sharing one planet: The events of 9/11, the suffering of our fellow humans in Darfur, the battles in Iraqi streets—we experience these in real time.

This revolution is also exploding our access to knowledge—and with it our power—as it helps dissolve the scarcity paradigm. Want a world-class education? Eighty-five percent of Massachusetts Institute of Technology course materials are now available free to anyone in the world through its "open course ware" at ocw.mit.edu. The site gets 1.5 million visits a month from all over the world. As professors' audiences explode, the quality of MIT teaching is improving, observes the system's director Anne Margulies. One hundred and ten universities worldwide are following MIT's lead and opening themselves to the world.

Flouting the top-down control characteristic of Thin Democracy, this revolution thrives on people's need to contribute and cooperate. Case in point? The widening embrace of Linux—an open source operating system—and nascent rejection of Microsoft, with its top-down control of 90 percent of the world's software market. A few years ago Munich, Germany, decided to convert thousands of government computers to Linux despite pleas by Microsoft's chief executive. Soon Brazil's government was on board, too, saving millions.

Founder of the open software movement that created Linux, Richard Stallman, said this about why he left the proprietary, top-down control software world: In that world, "the first step in using a computer was to promise not to help your neighbor. A cooperating community was forbidden. The rule made by the owners of proprietary software was, 'If you share with your neighbor, you are a pirate.'"

So Stallman created the opposite: software rules and culture that encourages mutual help and mutual learning. And it's catching on.

An icon in the demystification of knowledge—and its cooperative creation by volunteer users just wanting to contribute—is of course Wikipedia, with seven million articles in two hundred fifty-one languages, fourteen times the articles in the Encyclopedia Britannica. When *Nature* magazine compared science articles in the two for accuracy, it found on average four errors in Wikipedia and three in Encyclopedia Britannica.[101]

The communications revolution—with independent news services proliferating online and independent documentaries showing up in mainstream theaters—is also emboldening citizens. In what could be this electoral season's prize understatement, John Edward's Internet strategist Matthew Gross told NPR in 2007, "Candidates no longer control the message." Think blogs, cell phone videos, podcasts, and YouTube.

New technologies are also making life tougher for officials keeping secrets, while for truth tellers, life is getting easier.

Consider Daniel Ellsberg.

Ellsberg became a hero for my generation when in 1971 he leaked what became known as the Pentagon Papers, classified material proving government deceit about the war in Vietnam. It took him six weeks to secretly photocopy seven thousand pages, and material from the documents appeared in the *New York Times* three whole months after they were received.

Contrast Ellsberg's effort with that of Treasury Secretary Paul O'Neill. Fired by President Bush in 2002, he just walked out the door with a CD-ROM containing nineteen thousand documents, and some of the most revealing material almost immediately appeared on the Web.[102]

Big difference.

Transparency is the new buzzword, and the new communications tools suddenly transform theoretically available information into practically *useable* information.

You can visit scorecard.org, key in your ZIP code, and find out not only which companies are polluting your town but what they are spewing into your water and air. When I did this, I was in for a shock: A company I jog by regularly ranks among my county's top twenty polluters. This Web-based service is possible only because the 1986 Right-to-Know law required corporate disclosure of certain types of toxic chemicals. That info went into an accessible online inventory.

In the first seven years after the inventory's 1988 launch, corporate releases of listed chemicals dropped by 45 percent,[103] and in the first fifteen, hazardous chemicals stored on-site fell almost 60 percent.[104] Here, required transparency alone—made useful because of the communications revolution—arguably produced history's fastest ever voluntary corporate environmental improvement.

2   A networking revolution.

Closely related, the Internet is also directly enabling citizen campaigns and enlivening global collaboration among citizen movements.

For starters, they become visible to one other: Environmentalist Paul Hawken's new Website wiserearth.org profiles over one hundred thousand citizen organizations in two hundred forty-three countries, still a small fraction of the total.

One moment in 1999 signaled the possibilities to come: It was the birth of "Indymedia," which was launched during the citizen protests against the World Trade Organization in Seattle. The online Independent Media Center had two million viewers in that first week, eclipsing visits to CNN. Using open-source software allowing anyone to publish, the center's sites—all known as "Indymedia"—have spread to more than a dozen countries. Its hub, now in eight languages, gets as many as one hundred thousand hits a day.

The power of citizen networking is just beginning to be felt. What those involved call "flexible networks of organizations," for example, achieved the 1997 Mine-Ban Treaty, and they abetted the success of the 2003 Global Tobacco Treaty, the world's first public health treaty mentioned earlier.

3   A revolution in human dignity.

The view that each human life is of inherent worth and thus entitled to a voice in our common destiny is still new, its consequences only now beginning to reverberate through our species.

Yet it's easy to miss how new and revolutionary this change is. Even in many of today's "old democracies" women won the right to vote so recently that some alive today were born without it. And just since 1980, citizens in forty-seven more countries have gained democratic rights, says a U.N. report.[105]

Other signs of this revolution? The new International Criminal court. With one hundred and four member countries (but not the United States), it's now prosecuting four crimes-against-humanity cases, including two Sudanese for the Darfur genocide. Also, the right to food—essential to human dignity—is now enshrined in the constitutions of twenty-two nations. And, in Europe, individuals believing their human rights to have been violated, without proper redress within their own nation, now have a place to turn. It is the supra-national European Court of Human Rights, a Strasbourg-based tribunal to which any state body of the forty-six country signatories can also bring a claim. In its current form just since 1998, the Court has issued judgments that range from holding the Russian military responsible for torturing Chechens to compensation for a Polish woman barred from ending her pregnancy even though giving birth, doctors told her, could leave her disabled (and did).

I'll understand if you think it's a stretch to claim a "revolution in human dignity" in a world experiencing genocide: or in a world where twelve to twenty-seven million people, nearly half of them children, are enslaved—forced to work by threat of violence for little or nothing; or where human trafficking is a booming $32 billion business.

Yet, slavery fighter Kevin Bales sees change: "[W]e don't have to win the moral argument; no one is trying to justify it any more."[106] That's a revolution.

4   An ecological revolution.

The fourth wind in the sails of Living Democracy also involves our consciousness—ecological imagery seeping deep into us over the last four decades and with profound effect. We're coming to see that ecology is not about "nature" apart from us. We and the butterflies are in this together. And such lovely metaphors suddenly become very real—and not so lovely—when we learn that, for example, on some days almost one-quarter of pollutants in Los Angeles air come from coal plants and cars in China and dust from deforestation in Asia.[107]

Ecological consciousness also tells us there is no "away" to which we can toss used goods. And there is no escape, either: The damage we create as we heat the planet or deny basic food and health care to billions is damage to our ecological and social tissue that *none* can avoid. Now, there's motivation.

Through ecology's lens, we can perceive our power in new ways, too, as I take up in the coming chapter. Since interdependence isn't a nice wish, *it is what is*, there can be no single action, isolated and contained. All actions create ripples—not just downward through hierarchical flows but outward globally through webs of connectedness. And we never know what those ripples might be. Beneath our awareness, perhaps, we are coming to realize that our acts do matter, all of them, everywhere, all the time.

Yeah, yeah, each action counts but we still must choose, I can hear a reader sighing. Do I engage right in my own backyard like the Kansans who began the chapter? Or do I go national—helping, say, to purge money's corrupting grip from politics with the Just6Dollars folks? Or what about climate chaos—it's global?

Local vs. national vs. global—this frame gets us nowhere. Rules of our economy and of politics set nationally, and globally, now divide and disempower people locally; yet many of us will become convinced that these rules can be made fair only as we experience change right in our own communities. There is no chicken or egg—all have to be happening at once. And are. The challenge is not the "level" of our engagement but whether our choices fire our passions and reverse the spiral of powerlessness—an exploration at the heart of Chapter 9.

But given the incessant stoking of fear in our society and the top-down control built into Thin Democracy, where is our power for this radical assertion of basic common sense? To discover it, we may have to rethink the meaning of power, too.

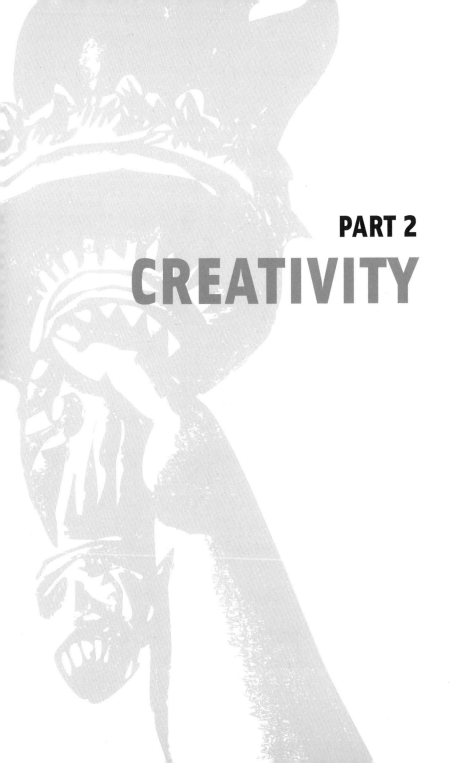

PART 2

CREATIVITY

4 POWER INVISIBLE

A Massachusetts teacher I once knew asked his tenth graders to blurt out the first words that came to mind on hearing the word "power." They said, "money," "parents," "guns," "bullies," "Adolf Hitler," and "Mike Tyson." And in my workshops with adults, I've heard similar words, plus "fist," "law," "corrupt," and "politicians." Often "men" pops out, too.

As long as we conceive of power as the capacity to exert one's will over another, it is something to be wary of. Power can manipulate, coerce, and destroy. And as long as we are convinced we have none, power will always look negative. Even esteemed journalist Bill Moyers recently reinforced a view of power as categorically negative. "The further you get from power," he said, "the closer you get to the truth."[108]

But power means simply our capacity to act. "Power is necessary to produce the changes I want in my community," Margaret Moore of Allied Communities of Tarrant (ACT) in Fort Worth, Texas, told me. I've found many Americans returning power to its original meaning—"to be able." From this lens, we each have power—and often, much more power than we think.

ONE CHOICE WE DON'T HAVE

In fact, we have no choice about whether to be world changers. If we accept ecology's insights that we exist in densely woven networks, as just noted, then we must also accept that every choice we make sends out ripples, even if we're not consciously choosing. *So the choice we have is not whether, but only how, we change the world.* All this means that public life is not simply what officials and other "big shots" have, as I've tried to capture in Chapter 2.

One related evidence of our power is so obvious it is often overlooked.

Human beings show up in *radically* different notches on the "ethical scale" depending on the culture in which we live. In Japan, "only" 15 percent of men beat their spouses. In many other countries, over half do. The murder rate in the United States is four times higher than in Western Europe, Canada, Australia, and Japan.

Plus, behavior can change quickly. Germany moved from a country in which millions of its citizens went along with mass murder to become in a single generation one of the world's more respected nations. An incomparably less consequential but still telling example: In only a decade, 1992 to 2002, U.S. high school students who admitted to cheating on a test at least once in a year climbed by 21 percent to three-quarters of all surveyed.[109]

So what do these differences and the speed of change in behavior tell us? That it is *culture*, not fixed aspects of human nature, which largely determines the prevalence of cooperation or brutality, honesty or deceit. And since *we* create culture through our daily choices, then we do, each of us, wield enormous power.

Let me explore related, empowering findings of science that also confirm our power.

MIRRORS IN OUR BRAINS

Recent neuroscience reveals our interdependence to be vastly greater than we'd ever imagined.

In the early 1990s, neuroscientists were studying the brain activity of monkeys, particularly in the part of the brain's frontal lobe associated with distinct actions, such as reaching or eating. They saw specific neurons firing for specific activities. But then they noticed something they didn't expect at all: The very same neurons fired when a monkey was simply *watching* another monkey perform the action.

"Monkey see, monkey do" suddenly took on a whole new meaning for me. Since we humans are wired like our close relatives, when we observe someone else, our own brains are simultaneously experiencing at least something of what that person is experiencing. More recent work studying humans has borne out this truth.[110]

These copycats are called "mirror neurons," and their implications are staggering. We do walk in one another's shoes, whether we want to or not.

> [Our] intimate brain-to-brain link-up...lets us affect the brain—and so the body—of everyone we interact with, just as they do us.
>
> —DANIEL GOLEMAN,
> SOCIAL INTELLIGENCE: THE NEW SCIENCE OF HUMAN RELATIONSHIPS [111]

We literally experience and therefore co-create one another, moment to moment. For me, our "imprintability" is itself a source of hope. We can be certain that our actions, and perhaps our mental states, register in others. We change anyone observing us. That's power.

And we never know who's watching. Just think: It may be when we feel most marginalized and unheard, but still act with resolve, that someone is listening or watching and their life is forever changed.

As I form this thought, the face of Wangari Maathai comes to mind. A Kenyan, Wangari planted seven trees on Earth Day in Nairobi in 1977 to honor seven women environmental leaders there. Then, over two decades, she was jailed, humiliated, and beaten for her environmental activism, but her simple act ultimately sparked a movement in which those seven trees became forty *million*, all planted by village women across Kenya.

In the fall of 2004, when Maathai got the call telling her she had just won the Nobel Peace Prize, her first words were: "I didn't know anyone was listening." But clearly, a lot of people were beginning to listen, from tens of thousands of self-taught tree planters in Kenya to the Nobel committee sitting in Oslo.

From there I flash back to a conversation with João Pedro Stédile, a founder of the largest and perhaps most effective social movement in this hemisphere—Brazil's Landless Workers' Movement, enabling some of world's poorest people to gain nearly twenty million acres of unused land. Under Brazil's military regime in the early 1980s even gathering a handful of people was risky. And, in that dangerous time, who helped motivate João Pedro? It was Cesar Chavez, he told me, and the U.S. farm workers.

I'll bet Chavez never knew.

Just as important, the findings of neuroscience also give us insight as to how to change and empower ourselves. They suggest that a great way is to place ourselves in the company of those we want most to be like. For sure, we'll become more like them. Thus, whom we choose as friends, as partners, whom we spend time with—these may be our most important choices. And "spending time" means more than face-to-face contact. What we witness on TV, in films, and on the Internet, what we read and therefore imagine—all are firing mirror neurons in our brains and forming us.

As the author of *Diet for a Small Planet*, I'm associated with a focus on the power of what we put into our mouths. But what we let into our minds equally determines who we become. So why not choose an empowering news diet? I've included my own menu suggestions in *Recommended Reading* at the book's end.

POWER ISN'T A FOUR-LETTER WORD

Power is an idea. And in our culture it's a stifling idea. We're taught to see power as something fixed—we either have it, or we don't. But if power is our capacity to get things done, then even a moment's reflection tells us we can't create much alone.

IDEA 3: Rethinking Power	
POWER IS	**POWER CAN BE**
Zero-sum. It strengthens some people at the expense of others. It divides what already exists.	Mutually expanding. It builds the capacities of all involved. It is creative, generating new strengths and new possibilities.
A one-way force: either you have it, or you don't. Life boils down to the powerful versus the powerless.	A give-and-take, two-way relationship. No one is ever completely powerless because each person's actions affect others.
Limiting, intimidating, and scary.	Freeing.
Controlling.	Collaborative.
Rigid, static.	Dynamic, always changing.
Derived mostly from laws, status, force, and wealth.	Derived from relationships, knowledge, experience, numbers, organization, creativity, vision, perseverance, discipline, humor, and more.
All about what I can do or get right now.	Mindful of creating and sustaining relational power over time.

From there, power becomes something we human beings develop together—*relational power*. And it's a lot more fun.

"Relational" suggests that power can expand for many people simultaneously. It's no longer a harsh, zero-sum concept —the more for you, the less for me. The growth in one person's power can enhance the power of others. *Idea 3* contrasts our limited, negative view of power with a freeing, relational view.

Let me tell you one story of relational power.

In the 1970s, pollution in Chattanooga, Tennessee, was so bad that drivers had to turn on headlights at noon to cut through it. But in the 1990s, this once-charming city—famous for its choo-choos—went from racially-divided ugly duckling to swan, winning international awards and the envy of its neighbors.

The city's rebirth sprang in part from big investments in the city's cultural renewal—including the world's largest freshwater aquarium, attracting over a million visitors a year; a renovated theater involving one thousand volunteers annually; and a new riverfront park.

But all these weren't the city fathers' ideas.

Twenty years ago, fifty spunky, frustrated citizens declared that the old ways of making decisions weren't working and drew their fellow residents—across race and class lines—into a twenty-week series of brainstorming sessions they called "visioning."

Their goal was hardly modest—to save their city by the end of the century. They called it Vision 2000. They drew up thirty-four goals, formed action groups, sought funding, and rolled up their sleeves.

By 1992, halfway along, the Visioners had already achieved a remarkable 85 percent of their goals. Smog was defeated, tourism was booming thanks to the new aquarium, crime was down, and jobs and low-income housing were on the rise. People stayed downtown after dark, and the refurbished riverside had become an oak-dappled mecca.

Chattanoogans didn't stop there. In 1992, a citywide meeting to shape a school reform agenda drew not the small crowd expected but fifteen hundred people, who generated two thousand suggestions.

By now the approach has seeped its way into the city's culture. In 2002, to plan a big waterfront project, three hundred people participated in a "charrette" where teams used rolls of butcher paper to draw what they wanted to see happen.

"Basically, everything we do, any major initiative in Chattanooga, now involves public participation," said Karen Hundt, who works for a joint city-county planning agency. From Atlanta to West Springfield, Massachusetts, from Bahrain to Zimbabwe, citizens taken by Chattanooga's story are rewriting it to suit their own needs.

Here power is not a fixed pie to be sliced up. It grows as citizens join together, weaving relationships essential to sustained change.

RELATIONAL POWER'S UNDER-APPRECIATED SOURCES

While we commonly think of power in the form of official status or wealth or force restricted to a few of us, take a moment to mull over these twelve sources of relational power available to any one of us:[112]

- *Building relationships of trust.* Thirty-five hundred congregations—Catholics, Protestants, Jews, and some Evangelicals and Muslims—are dues-paying members of one hundred thirty-three religious networks nationwide. These local federations with members adding up to as many as three million Americans are successfully tackling problems that range from poverty wages to failing schools. Their genius is what they call "one-on-one" organizing strategies. These involve face-to-face meetings allowing ordinary people to discover their own capacities because someone—finally—is listening.

- *Ability to analyze power and self-interest.* One such organization, Communities Organized for Public Service in San Antonio, analyzes corporate interests before bringing corporations into dialogue on job-training reform.

- *Knowledge.* National People's Action documents banks' racial "redlining" in lending and helps to pass the federal Community Reinvestment Act, which has brought over a trillion dollars into poor neighborhoods. Workers at South Mountain Company in Massachusetts buy the company and apply knowledge from their direct experience to make it profitable and to incorporate energy efficient methods.

- *Numbers of people.* The congregation-based Industrial Areas Foundation is able to gather together thousands for public "actions," commanding the attention of lawmakers.

- *Discipline.* Young people in the Youth Action Program—precursor to the nationwide YouthBuild—handle themselves with such decorum at a New York's City Council meeting that officials are moved to respond to the group's request for support.

- *Vision.* In the Merrimack Valley Project in Massachusetts, some businesses "catch" the citizens' vision of industry responsive to community values and change their positions.

- *Diversity.* Memphis's Shelby County Interfaith organization identifies distinct black and white interests on school reform and multiplies its impact by addressing both sets in improving Memphis schools.

- *Creativity.* Citizens in St. Paul devise their own neighborhood network to help the elderly stay out of nursing homes. Regular folks in San Antonio devise a new job training program that's become a national model.

- *Persistence.* Members of ACORN, a two hundred twenty-five thousand-member-strong, low-income people's organization, stand in line all night to squeeze out paid banking lobbyists for seats in the congressional hearing room debating the Community Reinvestment Act.

- *Humor.* Kentuckians for the Commonwealth stage a skit at the state capitol. In bed are KFTC members portraying legislators and their farmer chairperson pretending to be a coal lobbyist. They pass big wads of fake cash under the covers. Grabbing media attention, they get their reform measure passed.

- *Chutzpah—Nerve.* Sixth graders in Amesville, Ohio, don't trust the EPA to clean up after a toxic spill in the local creek, so they form themselves into the town's water quality control team and get the job done.

- *Mastering the arts of democracy.* Organizations of the Industrial Area Foundation network, over fifty nationwide, evaluate and reflect—often right on the spot—following each public action or meeting. They ask: How do you feel? How did each spokesperson do? Did we meet our goals? A seasoned organizer will also try to teach a lesson about what the organization sees as the "universals" of public life, such as relational power.

DROPS COUNT

Sadly, though, many of us remain blind to such a promising reframing of possibility. Imagining ourselves powerless, we disparage our acts as mere drops in the bucket…as, well, useless. But think about it: Buckets fill up really fast on a rainy night. Feelings of powerlessness come *not* from seeing oneself as a drop; they arise when we can't perceive the bucket at all. Thus, to uproot feelings of powerlessness, we can work to define and shape the bucket—*to consciously construct a frame that gives meaning to our actions.*

That satisfying exploration begins, I believe, when we recognize that our planet's multiple crises are neither separate nor random. They flow largely from a partial, and thus distorted, view of our own nature, which leads us to turn our fate over to forces outside our control, especially to a one-rule economy violating deep human sensibilities, not to mention our common sense. Our deepening crises flow, as well, as I take up in Chapter

8, from humanity's to-date lack of preparedness to identify and skillfully to confront the tiny minority among us who seem to lack empathetic sensibilities.

As you now know, for me a "bucket" that both contains and gives meaning to our creative, positive acts is Living Democracy. It springs from and meets humanity's common and deep emotional and spiritual needs. So, I wonder: In a world torn apart by sectarian division, could Living Democracy become a uniting *civic* vision complementing our religious and spiritual convictions—a nonsectarian yet soul-satisfying pathway out of the current morass?

I can't be certain, of course, but I think so.

And then again, I ask myself often, *whatever* the real odds of reversing our global catastrophe, is there a more invigorating way to live than that of making democracy a way of life?

In answering that question negatively, I *am* certain.

5 THE ART OF POWER

I wonder whether Americans still believe liberty has to be learned and that its skills are worth learning. Or have they been deluded by two centuries of rhetoric into thinking that freedom is 'natural' and can be taken for granted?
—BENJAMIN BARBER, AUTHOR, *STRONG DEMOCRACY;*
DIRECTOR, CIVWORLD[113]

With the collapse of the Soviet Union in 1989, those outside marveled at the staggering pace of change there. Communism's political institutions—seemingly as rigid and immovable as the mammoth steel and cement structures that housed them—simply collapsed. Command economies gave way to the market. And the world celebrated when democracy seemed to be breaking out all over.

Yet as the 1990s wore on and the euphoria wore off, it became clear that behind these highly visible structural changes, the reality of people's daily lives was in many ways worsening quickly. Even life expectancy began to fall. The KGB, the feared Soviet secret police, didn't dissolve exactly; it morphed into the Russian FSB that many have experienced as a state-sanctioned mafia.

Similarly, consider the tragic consequences of the U.S. invasion of Iraq, ostensibly to "bring democracy." With no appreciation of, or attention to, the values and norms that make democracy work, the U.S. occupation instead unleashed a nightmare of internecine violence.

Formal institutions can change dramatically, but that is not enough. Something else is needed.

But what is that something else?

It's not nearly as clear-cut or visible as the structures of government or the rules on the books. But that something else may be just as important to democracy. (After all, the old Soviet Union had a superb bill of rights...on paper.)

I call what's needed the *culture of democracy.*

As noted in the previous chapter, it is culture's power, not law, that explains so much of our social existence—why Western Europe, for instance, can register a GDP per person only two-thirds of that of the United States and still enjoy quality of life measures exceeding ours.[114] Why teen pregnancy rates here are four times those in France and Germany.[115]

To a large extent, culture is a set of expectations. How will we behave toward one another? What can we expect from our fellow citizens? What does the community expect of us? What are the unspoken rules that we just assume will be followed in our daily interactions? In one sense, a culture of democracy can be defined as one that builds trust.

Reading that last sentence, one's reaction might understandably be: Trust? Forget it. Sales of locks, guns, and gates are booming. True, as fear is stoked, trust shrinks, but reflecting even for a moment, we realize that trust is still ubiquitous. Maybe, like cooperation, so ubiquitous we don't register it. Every time we put a bite of food in our mouths, we put our lives into the hands of a supply chain of strangers. Every time the light turns green and we press the gas pedal, we trust strangers also capable of doing us great harm.

Societies couldn't function without trust. The challenge now is re-creating and deepening trust by engaging directly with others to create a culture that works for all of us.

DEMOCRACY'S ARTS

The people from all walks of life you meet in this book are shaping a democratic culture offering them much greater rewards. At the same time they're strengthening personal qualities that, in turn, make them even more effective. Skills that make possible this self-reinforcing pattern I call the arts of democracy. *Idea 4* lists ten of these, and on our Website is a fuller "how-to" guide.[116]

I choose the term "art" quite deliberately, seeking to elevate the notion of democratic practice to something that is prized. "Art" doesn't have to suggest something exclusive at which only the talented few can succeed. Developing an art is possible for each of us, but it can't be learned by rote or formula. In any art, individuals add their own twists; and its practice calls on not one but many of our faculties.

Most important, an art can be learned. In fact, there is no end to the learning.

IDEA 4: Ten Arts of Democracy

ART ONE: ACTIVE LISTENING
Encouraging the speaker and searching for meaning

ART TWO: CREATIVE CONFLICT
Confronting others in ways that produce growth

ART THREE: MEDIATION
Facilitating interaction to help people in conflict hear one another

ART FOUR: NEGOTIATION
Problem solving that meets some key interests of all involved

ART FIVE: POLITICAL IMAGINATION
Re-imaging our futures according to our values

ART SIX: PUBLIC DIALOGUE
Public talk on matters that concern us all

ART SEVEN: PUBLIC JUDGMENT
Public decision making that allows citizens to make choices they are willing to help implement

ART EIGHT: CELEBRATION
Expressing joy and gratitude for what we learn as well as what we achieve

ART NINE: EVALUATION AND REFLECTION
Assessing and incorporating the lessons we learn through action

ART TEN: MENTORING
Supportively guiding others in learning these arts of public life

THE POWER OF SIMPLY LISTENING

The first art of old-style politics or old-style management is drawing up one's manifesto, plan, or agenda and then selling it to others. The first art of Living Democracy is simply listening.

But is it really so simple?

At its most complete, active listening suggests putting oneself in another's shoes, seeing the world—even if for just a fleeting moment—from the other's vantage point. We can then begin to perceive links to our own interests, making common action possible.

Earlier I recounted how COPS (Communities Organized for Public Service), a citizen organization in San Antonio, reacted to its frustration at high unemployment rates among Hispanics. COPS members were upset because their city's biggest employers were bringing in outsiders to fill local jobs.

COPS might have simply staged an angry protest. Instead, they invited corporate leaders to the table. COPS members listened. They listened to the concerns of those they might have seen only as adversaries. They listened to the companies' CEOs tell them of their own frustrations in not being able to find qualified employees locally. COPS members discovered a common interest with the business leaders: improving the city's job training efforts. From there, COPS went on to develop an innovative redesign of the city's job training programs, which the city council passed unanimously.

Active listening also spurs creativity.

That's why English professor Peter Elbow at the University of Massachusetts uses active listening as a teaching tool. He calls it "The Believing Game." Our culture overemphasizes the importance of critical thinking, Peter believes. We're taught to find flaws in *any* argument. But this approach can make even the *best* idea look bad, so a creative idea with far-reaching advantages can get ignored just because it contradicts conventional wisdom or is poorly stated.

To avoid this risk, Peter argues, we can learn to make a conscious, disciplined effort to *pretend* a new idea is the best proposal, and then see what we notice.[117]

What's required is a special kind of active listening—the temporary suspension of disbelief. Dropping our tendency to first identify problems frees our creativity.

Active listening changes the speaker, too.

In private life, when we go to a friend for advice and that friend simply listens, we're often amazed to discover it is we ourselves who have the answers. We may have had them all along, but formulating our ideas to make ourselves clear to someone else enables us suddenly to "see" those answers for the first time.

The same possibility exists in public life. In North Carolina, for example, the Listening Project bases its community improvement work on hundreds of in-depth, one-on-one interviews with people in their homes. Instead of quick check-off surveys, organizers ask open-ended questions about people's values and concerns. In one home, a middle-aged white man complained that the biggest problem he saw was the noisy black teenagers who hung out on the streets and caused trouble.

On a simple survey, that one comment might have gotten him labeled a racist. But the organizers just listened. They didn't argue. As the man talked, he began to reflect, as well. By the end of the interview, he himself had restated—and re-understood— his neighborhood's problem as its lack of decent recreational and job opportunities for young people.

So while we think of listening as passive, this story suggests much more. The very act of truly being listened to can profoundly change the speaker.

CONFLICT AS CREATIVE

Living Democracy means ongoing change, and change implies, minimally, that somebody thinks we can improve on the status quo. No big shock, then, that somebody else feels criticized. So change entails conflict. Gradually, therefore, it's dawned on me that one of the biggest obstacles to Living Democracy is a quality I personally have. Hmmm.

My own fear of conflict is pretty common; at least there's some personal solace there. While Americans flock to action movies and stay glued to soaps drenched with melodrama, in real life, most of us abhor conflict. I am convinced it's not just fear of a bruised ego; it's a primal fear of losing standing in our "tribe," of being cast out into the wilderness, as I return to in Chapter 8.

Our aversion to conflict pops out in the sentiments of parents who brag about their "good kids" who "never give me problems." Or school principals whose extra praise is reserved for teachers maintaining the most obedient classrooms. Or bosses who make clear that it's those that "don't make waves" who'll be rewarded.

Fear of bucking these messages stops us from acting on what we know we want. So creatively *using* conflict is a key to creating the societies we want. That seems pretty clear, and it's why I'm impressed by sophisticated citizen organizations that train and mentor in this art of democracy.

They are teaching that conflict means engagement—that something real is in motion. It's an opening, not a closing.

The national grassroots organization ACORN runs a training institute for members, and the huge congregation-based Industrial Areas Foundation network make rehearsing and re-rehearsing for any contentious public encounter part of its M.O.

In Massachusetts, the two thousand members of Lawrence CommunityWorks—bringing life back to what once was a thriving industrial town—have created their own members' training program. It's called the Poder ("to be able" in Spanish) Institute. The group's organizing director Alma Couverthié described the impetus to me: "As more and more people got involved through our Neighbor Circles [series of three dinners in which neighbors discuss common concerns], they realized they needed more tools. So our classes run every Saturday afternoon for six months. So far sixty people have completed the course."

Using what it calls "network organizing," this community development corporation doesn't focus on bricks-and-mortar rebuilding. It looks for "organic connections" among people and then invests in strengthening and multiplying them. It's out of these relationships that the rebuilding comes. "Embedded in our teaching [building on Paulo Freire's *Pedagogy of the Oppressed* and more] is our understanding that conflict can be used for good and is necessary for growth," Alma told me.

She then described her response to a workshop on conflict put on by national trainers who didn't share her philosophy. "The leader started by telling us that conflict was to be avoided at all costs." At that point "I raised my hand to object," she said. "Finally, I just left."

Apparently, Alma herself knew how to practice what she was preaching.

In Des Moines, Iowa, several years ago Sally Riggs got involved with Iowa Citizens for Community (Iowa CCI) after her family had been deceived by a predatory lender.

She was reluctant at first, but with coaching, Sally gained confidence and skills.

"Before the meetings [with the mortgage company] I used to feel like I was going to be sick, I was so nervous. But the rehearsals helped. We would go to the group's office and practice making our case in their old meeting room. Joe or Tyler, staff organizers, would play the part of the executive across the table. They'd throw at us all the arguments we thought they would use. We did that as often as we could, and then, an hour before the real meeting, we would do it one last time. There weren't too many meetings when something came up that we hadn't seen coming and got ourselves ready for."

All this worked for Sally when her big day came in Chicago. When one financial executive seemed to dismiss her argument, Sally was hardly tongue-tied. She recalls saying: "And how would you like it if your five-year-old girl couldn't answer the phone in her own home because she was scared to?"

While she had always been petrified of the mortgage company, that changed when a bus full of other victims and supporting members of Iowa CCI refused to leave the office of one of the worst lenders. The police, summoned by the executives, advised the cowering mortgage execs that perhaps they should solve the problems of the people in their office. They did.

Naturally, we fear power imbalances. If our adversary is someone we perceive as holding power by his or her very position, how do we balance it out? With both the power of knowledge we bring in the door and the power of our numbers—the strength we communicate and we feel by having allies at our side.

KIDS LEARN CONFLICT IS OKAY

Although conflict in schools that spirals into ugly violence grabs the headlines, thousands of schools are learning to deter violence and turn conflict into strength.

They train both students and teachers to mediate differences among their peers in a movement unheard of only twenty years ago. It works this way: students volunteer for mediation training—typically fifteen hours covering active listening, paraphrasing, reframing, and role playing. The new mediators promote their services and encourage their peers to bring unresolved disputes to them. Schools often find many more students volunteering than they can use.

"One teacher typically becomes the point person," Richard Cohen, a founder of the movement, explained to me. "When a conflict arises, this person chooses two students who might be right for those two parties. Some schools handle three hundred to four hundred cases a year, and a mature program reaches 10 percent of the student body each year."

In only a decade, the number of participating schools has jumped from five thousand to between ten and fifteen thousand.

"In a new high school in Lincoln-Sudbury, Massachusetts, they even built into the plans a suite of rooms specifically for mediation," Richard said. "That's how far we've come.

"What I love about mediation training is that it puts students themselves in charge of an aspect of school that is so important to them—their relationships. And all types, not just the honor roll students, are involved.

We teach kids that conflict is normal, that there's no way to avoid it, and that it can be positive.

—RICHARD COHEN, FOUNDER, SCHOOL MEDIATION ASSOCIATES

"It's not unusual to find that the average student is a better mediator than the adult. Effectiveness depends on being good at reading people, making them comfortable. You can get a seventeen-year-old with a ton of that kind of interpersonal intelligence," Richard explained.

"We ask kids whether they've ever felt closer to someone *after* going through a conflict. And a lot of hands go up. They get it. We also teach that conflict can be resolved cooperatively, not always competitively."

As with many breakthroughs creating a culture of Living Democracy, school mediation now has a long enough track record to measure its success. A 2003 report shows that in more than nine in ten cases, school mediation achieves a resolution, and disputants express satisfaction at almost as high a rate.[118]

As we learn to practice the arts of democracy, it may hit us that engagement is not, as we've been told, the spinach we must eat to move on to the dessert of personal freedom. Rather, it feels like another way of talking about the unending personal growth that makes life worth living. Or, as one feisty citizen expressed it to me: "The fun of power."

6 TALKING DEMOCRACY

We have a language of Marxism and we have a language
of capitalism, but we have no language of democracy.
And we cannot create what we cannot name.

—HISTORIAN LAWRENCE GOODWYN

Throughout this book, I've stressed the power of "frame," the lens through which we interpret our world. But what creates our frame? Largely, it's language—the words and metaphors we use every day.

Progressives groan that over the last three decades the Far Right has spun together its own language, creating a frame that resonates across the heartland. "Family values," "leave us alone," "it's your money," "tax-and-spend Liberals"—all of these phrases create frames of meaning. Yet many Americans who worry about their negative power continue to use terms that fail to communicate a positive alternative. Worse, their terms are heard by others to mean the opposite of what the speaker intends.

In "getting a grip," a big piece of the challenge is disciplining ourselves to find and use words that convey a new frame, one that spreads a sense of possibility and helps people see emerging signs of Living Democracy that fuel the Spiral of Empowerment.

To underscore why I believe language is so important, let me toss out a few current, deadly terms and propose alternatives. My goal is to get us thinking, arguing, defining, and ultimately determined to stick to words that communicate what we really mean.

GLOBALIZATION OR GLOBAL CORPORATE POWER?

To most Americans, globalization equals great Indian food, cool music from Mali, and cheap jeans from China. Economist Joseph Stiglitz in *Globalization and Its Discontents* defines globalization as "the closer integration of the countries and peoples of the world."[119]

Who in their right mind would oppose that?

Pulitzer-winning columnist Thomas Friedman tells us that the current stage of globalization is "shrinking the world from size small to size tiny."[120] Distances are evaporating, he suggests. How positive! And even to those who lament the downside of outsourcing, this increasingly interconnected world is unstoppable.

But the term *globalization* focuses attention narrowly on the *scope* of activity. It diverts us from asking who is in *control* of that activity and therefore who benefits.

In other words, "globalization" jumps right over the question of power. Its defenders swoon over growing interdependence—suggesting mutuality in power relations. But reality, propelled by one-rule economics, is deepening *de*pendence—that is, widening power imbalances as more and more people are forced to live with the consequences of decisions made by distant boards of global corporations and by decision makers from the International Monetary Fund to the World Trade Organization, dominated by corporate interests.

Putting the power question front and center, what if we were consistently to link the term globalization to centralizing corporate control?

"Corporate globalization" or "global corporate power"—both better capture what is really going on. These terms begin to alert listeners that the power of governments—of which one hundred twenty-two out of one hundred ninety-two are now elected and therefore at least nominally accountable to citizens—is giving way (or being given away) to centralizing corporate power, directed by unelected boards and managers accountable (at best) only to shareholders.

And what about those movements countering global corporate power? What do we call them?

In the corporate media, they are "anti-globalization activists," which probably strikes most people as knee-jerk negative and utterly futile. But we can make clear that our vision is the essence of realism; it's globalizing corporate control that's unsustainable. So let us self-identify instead as "pro-democracy advocates." Or, even better, as "living democracy advocates."

FREE MARKET-FREE TRADE OR FAIR MARKET-FAIR TRADE?

From the International Forum on Globalization to the World Social Forum, progressives rail against "free market" policies.

Wrong enemy. The free market is no more real than the tooth fairy.

"There isn't one grain of anything in the world that is sold in a free market. Not one! The only place you see a free market is in the speeches of politicians."[121] So said not an irate farmer but the CEO of the agribusiness giant Archer Daniels Midland. He should know: his company, and others including Cargill and Tate & Lyle, have paid over $1 billion to settle price-fixing lawsuits.[122]

Markets are either fair or unfair; they are never "free" or "unfettered"—i.e., functioning on their own without rules. Today market rules, and there are plenty, are written to serve the interests of global corporations: The full text of the North American Free Trade Agreement runs to seventeen hundred pages. Open, fair markets result not from keeping "hands off" but from creating fair rules democratically.

As we've seen, today's single-rule economics—highest return to existing wealth, i.e. shareholders and CEOs—inexorably concentrates wealth and power, undermining competitive markets. It takes democracy—real, living democracy—to shape and enforce rules to keep wealth and power widely distributed—from progressive taxation to a floor under wages to anti-trust enforcement—so that markets stay fair and open. And it takes living democracy—citizens deliberating over shared values—to decide what should and should not be a market commodity in the first place.

So let's banish "free trade" and "free market" from our lips. And let's clarify that it's not progressives who are anti-market. Hardly. Actually, it's the ideology of Thin Democracy, taken as gospel by the

Far Right, that kills markets. Thin Democracy's concentrating wealth destroys competition and closes market access to all but the better off.

REGULATIONS OR STANDARDS?

I hear "regulation," and I stiffen: I think constraint, Big Brother, red tape, inefficiency. On the other hand, most of us warm to the idea of standards; we especially love "high standards." So in addressing our needs as citizens for clean air, water, and soil, for example, what if we were to substitute "standards" every time "regulation" started to pop out of our mouths?

So in 2006, Maine didn't pass new "regulations" requiring electronic manufacturers to take responsibility for recycling TVs and computer monitors, as I discuss in Chapter 9. No, Maine raised the bar, embracing a higher standard, one in which an industry is now responsible for the life cycle of what it produces.

Sounds really different, doesn't it?

CONSUMERS OR BUYERS?

The very idea of "consumer" is a big handicap to thinking straight—err, I mean thinking circularly. The word falsely conveys that what we purchase disappears from the ecosystem. But actually, we consume nothing at all. There is no "away" to which we can throw our stuff. That's the heart of what the ecological awakening teaches us, yet the word "consumer" continues our slumber, keeping our eyes closed to the consequences of our choices.

More accurate terms are "buyer," "purchaser," or "user." Using them, we're reminded that we are simply a pass-through in a conversion process: Our "stuff" moves from extraction and processing to another state—and that state is either destructive pollution *or* re-use and, ultimately, healthful integration back into the wider ecosystem.

Examining words like "consumer" versus "buyer" or "free trade" versus "fair trade" reminds us that a single term can carry within it a whole worldview—either blinding or clarifying. They can keep us stuck or open us to possibility. Consider trying out the new terms, paying attention to the feelings that arise as you use them. Invent better, more precise ones to aid the emergence of more life-serving mental frames.

Talking democracy is, of course, not just about choosing specific words to better convey what we mean. It is about engaging in conversation about what matters most to us—and with people who may not share our views. That's why I love the motto of Conversation Cafés: "Tired of small talk? Try some big talk." Check it out at conversationcafe.org.

Meetup.org is another great tool through which to encounter people to explore the questions and entry points in this book. The Study Circles Resource Center, scrc.org, which opened Chapter 3, helps communities use deep dialogue to solve problems.

To explore the rich world of democratic dialogue, a great place to start is the National Coalition for Dialogue and Deliberation, at thataway.org.

Enjoy.

Idea 5: Toward a Language of Democracy
"How forcible are right words." —Job 15:25

WIDELY USED TERMS	CONFUSING CONNOTATIONS	ALTERNATIVES TO COMMUNICATE MORE ACCURATELY & POWERFULLY
Activist	Rabble-rouser, extremist with own agenda	Engaged citizen, active citizen, empowered citizen
Anti-globalization	Backward, selfish, isolationist	Pro-democracy, pro-strong communities, anti-corporate control, anti-economic concentration
Citizenship	Burden, duty, boring	Public engagement, community building
Conventional farming	Sounds benign and time-tested, when it is neither	Chemically-dependent farming, extractive agriculture, factory farming
Conservatives	Implies devotion to preserving the environment and communities	Far Right, anti-democratic Right (when it applies)
Democracy	Limited to voting and government	Living Democracy: a way of living in which the democratic values of fairness, inclusion, and mutual accountability infuse all dimensions of our public lives.

Free trade	Implies absence of government control, an automatic mechanism. It doesn't exist.	Corporation-favoring trade, unfair trade
Globalization	Implies interdependence, more connection, free trade, cheaper goods	Global corporate control, global corporatism, economic centralization, economic feudalism, downward pressure on global wages
Social justice	Associated with radical Left, forced equality	Fairness, fair opportunity, freedom
Liberal	Favoring big government	Progressive, democratic
Minimum wage	Fails to convey human impact	Poverty wage vs. living wage
National debt, per person	Lacks meaning to most people	"Birth tax"—share of nation's debt each newborn faces, $150,000 in 2005[123]
Nonprofit organization	Defined in negative	Social-benefit organization, citizens' organization
Organic farming, Low-input	Focuses only on the absence of things— synthetic pesticides and fertilizers	Ecological farming: using the science of ecology to increase productivity and quality, while enhancing the environment; knowledge-intensive farming
Pro-choice	Sounds trivial	Pro-conscience*
Pro-life	Misleads: making abortion illegal doesn't prevent it.	For criminalizing abortion

Protest, demonstration	Limited, defensive	"Civic obedience"—positive act to defend democratic values
Public life	Restricted to officials and celebrities	What we each do as buyer, worker, employer, parent, voter, investor, and in all the other roles we play daily making huge ripples
Regulation	Big Brother, top-down intrusive government, inefficiency	Standards protecting ownership diversity, competition, health, and the environment; public protections; "values boundaries" within which the market serves community
Right to same-sex marriage	Focuses on sexuality	Freedom to marry, equal marriage
Taxes	Burden, rip-off of "our" money	Membership dues for a strong, healthy society; "the price of civilization," as Justice Oliver Wendell Holmes, Jr., put it
Welfare state	Coddling people, big bureaucracy	Fair-opportunity state

*My gratitude to Kathleen Kennedy Townsend for this term.

PART 3
COURAGE

7 SEIZE THE MOMENT

*In 1974 I would walk by people dying from famine to teach my
economics class at the university...And I said: 'What is this?'
I felt completely empty...The theories I was teaching were useless for
these dying people. I realized I could help people as a human being,
not as an economist. So I decided to become a basic human being ...I
no longer carried any pre-conceived notions.*

—DR. MUHAMMAD YUNUS, 2006 NOBEL PEACE PRIZE LAUREATE &
FOUNDER OF GRAMEEN BANK, BANGLADESH[124]

We humans see pretty much what we expect to see, I've
argued. We often can't even register what doesn't fit our
picture of how the world works. Yikes. If that's true, you may
well respond, how is it possible ever to change? Aren't we frozen
in self-destruct mode?

No, I don't think so. From my own life experiences and
from the extraordinary people I've met, certain insights about
breaking free are coming clear. I've witnessed people doing the
apparently impossible—perceiving the "screen" through which
they now peer, seeing with new eyes, then moving forward with
improved vision.

A DOWNWARD SPIN

But before exploring the possibility, let me recap the self-reinforcing downward spiral now trapping us—Thin Democracy's vicious cycle—which, I believe, we can learn to see and to escape. Follow the flow in the *Spiral of Powerlessness* inside the front cover suggesting that our materialistic, competitive culture denies deep needs that live within virtually all of us. I've mentioned our needs for fairness, for meaningful connection with others, for efficacy, and for meaning.

Most of us learn to deny that we're squelching such needs; maybe it is just too painful to acknowledge how much of ourselves we're giving up. But if these needs aren't met, most of us don't just roll over and pretend we don't have them; we seek their satisfaction in less-than-ideal ways.

Unable to satisfy our yearning for connection through common endeavor, we try the next best thing—to feel included because of our outer identities—wearing what's "in," choosing work we think will please our parents or bring us status.

Our yearning for power gets twisted, too. Power, as I've said, means our "capacity to act," but if we feel we can't make a dent positively, we go for control. If we feel put down at work or at home, not heard or seen, we're tempted to try to exert control over something—maybe our child, our spouse. In its extreme form, the response to thwarting our innate need for power is violence.

Psychiatrist and author James Gilligan has spent much of his long career working with violent criminals. He stresses the deep human need for acceptance and power, then tells us violence is sometimes the only avenue to respect that the men he treats see as available to them. He quotes a violent inmate in a running battle with correction officers: "...I've got to have my self-respect, and I've declared war on the whole world till I get it![125]

But not only do ersatz avenues for getting what we want fail to satisfy, they make things *worse*. Addictive eating can destroy our bodies, addictive shopping destroys our ecosystem, and attempts to control others create resistance and fear.

A vicious cycle moves into high gear as we strive harder, causing the gap between our inner needs and the reality outside to expand into a chasm. The bigger it gets, the more we cling to our ways, for at least they're familiar. No wonder it can seem impossible to break free of this destructive cycle that I try to capture in the cycle of fear in *Idea 6*.

IDEA 6: Inner World of Living Democracy

Experience Joy

in truer connection & greater efficacy

Ease Fear

by attracting and embracing new "tribes"

Glimpse Possibility

of more life-serving mental maps and follow curiosity

Find Entry Points

to act personally to shift causal patterns toward life

Cycle of **HOPE**

Recognize Fear

as a call to courage, not a verdict of failure

MOMENT OF DISSONANCE/ MOMENT OF OPPORTUNITY

Become conscious of disconnect between inner and outer worlds

Dominant mental map cracks

Fear expulsion from "tribe"

How do I respond?

Experience Fear

of acting on our need to create a world truer to our values

Cycle of **FEAR**

Feel Disconnect

between inner sense of fairness & empathy and the "real" world

Deny

our need for connection & efficacy and deny our denial!

Crises Worsen

citizens disengage; society & environment degrade further

Seek Substitutes

connection via consumption; efficacy via control & violence

Concepts explored in *Hope's Edge* (2002), *You Have the Power* (2004) *and Democracy's Edge* (2006). Adapted by Frances Moore Lappé and Richard Rowe, Small Planet Institute, www.smallplanetinstitute.org.

A RUDE SHOCK

Sometimes, though, we get lucky. We get a big helper. It can come as a kick in the pants, or what Bangladeshi Muhammad Yunus, quoted above, calls a "rude shock." His happened in the early 1970s after Yunus had returned to his starving, war-ravaged country to teach following a stint in a Tennessee university. His shock came the moment he admitted to himself that his classroom theories weren't helping, or maybe they were even hurting.

"Seize the moment" typically refers to a positive moment of opportunity, one not to be wasted. Gradually it's dawned on me, though, that such a moment can come as a disconcerting shock, dissonance that might not feel too good at the time. It is in these precious moments—when something shakes us up, rattling us from our resignation or depression, or galvanizing that vague sense that there must be more to life—that we can break free.

Dr. Yunus's moment of dissonance led him to drop his textbook theories and begin to listen to poor people themselves. He learned that their poverty was linked to their virtual servitude to money lenders, and his "aha" was the realization that credit, unavailable to poor people, could transform their lives. Bankers laughed at him. But his moment of dissonance led to an international microcredit movement that's since expanded to sixty countries, lifting tens of millions of people out of poverty.

And to a Nobel Peace Prize for Dr. Yunus.

One early moment of dissonance for me occurred sitting in an agricultural library, age twenty-six, astounded that the evidence of abundance of food worldwide clashed with headlines and textbooks, all warning of impending food shortages. I wanted to tell the world: Nature doesn't make hunger. Humans do!

I felt like the little boy in the fairy tale who says the emperor wears no clothes. I was scared, really scared—what if I'd misplaced a decimal point and gotten it all wrong? How could I be right and the grown-up "experts" mistaken?

But I couldn't turn back. I couldn't stay quiet.

Fortunately, we don't have to rely on accidental encounters to trigger these precious moments. We can each expose ourselves to people, ideas, and events that create internal dissonance—that feeling that something just doesn't fit right anymore.

I think, for example, of a couple who, in the fall of 2006, approached me to sign a book for their young daughter. We were gathered in the anteroom of a gorgeous Pittsburgh hotel ballroom after celebrating the work of a local social-benefit organization called Just Harvest, as well as that of the United Steel Workers.

A bit timidly at first, they told me they'd always felt comfortable as Republicans within a "conservative" Christian church, but earlier in the year a light had gone on for them: They had exposed themselves to new ideas and suddenly realized that the Bush administration had not leveled with Americans about Iraq and had led us into disaster there. With heavy hearts they shared their new perspective with their minister, himself a staunch defender of the administration.

The minister sternly warned the couple: Don't tell anyone else in the church, because they will turn against you. This "rude shock" jolted the couple out of a place of comfort. They had to choose, and they chose to engage with new ideas, new people.

As I listened, I felt emboldened by their courage and joyful that we were together that night, celebrating a group addressing the roots of hunger, one their church might have considered subversive. This family experienced the dissonance at the center of the Inner World of Living Democracy, in *Idea 6,* then broke away from a limiting frame and was free to discover new "tribes," easing the pain of separation and encouraging them to continue to grow within a cycle of hope.

In moments such as those this young family experienced, we each choose. Do we suppress the discomfort? Or do we listen to it, delve into the disconnect, making the leap necessary to put the world together in a new way?

To be sure, these are not once-in-a-lifetime moments. We'll have, if we're lucky, many such moments when we have to listen to our inner wisdom, question our path, and see with new eyes. Our hearts may be torn open. It may hurt, or it may be thrilling. But we know we can't turn back.

8 WHEN FEAR MEANS GO

The danger lies in refusing to face the fear...Courage is more
exhilarating than fear and in the long run it is easier.
—ELEANOR ROOSEVELT[126]

In these moments of dissonance, fear can always stop us dead in our tracks, for it has become the "emotional plague of our planet," observes French philosopher Patrick Viveret.

To break free, we must understand how we arrived here, and to do that, we must dig. The roots of this plague run deeper than our government's determination to turn a single heinous attack into a state of perpetual war or that of corporate advertisers to relentlessly fuel our insecurities.

To understand, we have to reach back in time. Way back.

Evolving eons ago within tightly knit tribes smack dab amidst species bigger and fiercer than us, we learned one lesson well: Alone, we don't stand a chance. So banishment meant sure death.

Humans are hardwired through eons of evolutionary experience to sense that our survival depends on staying on the "inside"—with the tribe. It shouldn't surprise us that scientists now report that our bodies experience the pain of being rejected as we do actual physical pain. We thrive on the approval of others; we dread humiliation above all else. So it's hard for human beings to say, "No, the whole pack is heading toward catastrophe!" We fear being cast out. So we hold back.

Yet our world's hyper-tribe *is* about to paddle over Victoria Falls—fouling air and water, speeding wealth's concentration, and building ever more weapons of mass destruction. In this situation, breaking from the pack means life.

Yet it *still* brings up instinctual fear.

Remember, though, that fear is in part an *idea,* and we know that ideas can trump instinct. Don't believe me? Consider "honor killings," in which fathers become murderers of daughters. Here an idea obviously trumps a primal instinct—parents' protection of offspring. Back to the positive, we can remake the idea of fear itself and reshape our instinctual responses. Based on my own experience and on hard science, I have come to believe that despite our biological heritage, we can *choose* how we respond to fear.

In fact, this may be the most important choice of our lives.

We can learn to reinterpret fear not as a verdict but as a signal. Whereas eons ago, breaking with the pack meant death, perhaps in today's circumstances it means just the opposite—it may be the only path to life.

With this insight, we can come to interpret our own body's fear sensations anew: Maybe they are not telling us that we're off track but that we are precisely where we should be—at our growth edge. We can see fear as pure energy, a tool we can work with.

FEAR AS PURE ENERGY

This possibility and the momentous consequences of this shift awakened for me one night in Nairobi, Kenya, as my daughter Anna and I recount in *Hope's Edge*. There, we met the Reverend Timothy Njoya, who had done something which until that evening I believed no human being could do.

For preaching a pro-democracy message despite the repeated threats against him by a dictatorial government, seven armed assailants appeared one night at his door. Despite all he'd been through, Reverend Njoya—a slight and agile man—playfully acted out for us what happened next. As he described his fingers being sliced off, his belly slashed open, he was chuckling!

...Me? My heart was beating wildly in my chest.

Then he told us that, as he lay on the floor and certain he was dying, he began to give his treasures away to his attackers—to one, his favorite Bible, to another, his library, and so on.

What!? I thought to myself. *How can this be? How could anyone not respond with sheer terror and life-preserving aggression to such brutality?*

So I asked: "But...Reverend Njoya, how were you not overcome by fear?"

Sitting deep in the cushioned armchair, his sweet face framed by a stiff white priest's collar, Reverend Njoya paused for only a moment. Then he said, "Fear is an energy that comes from inside us, not outside. It's neutral. So we can channel it into fear, paranoia, or euphoria, whatever we choose." He rose out of his chair.

"Imagine a lion," he said, crouching. "When a lion sees prey or predator, it senses fear first. But instead of lunging blindly in defense or in attack, it recoils." Reverend Njoya moved back, leaning on his left leg and crouching lower. "The lion pauses a moment, targets his energies. Then he springs.

"We can do the same. We can harness our would-be fears, harmonize our energies, and channel them into courage." His whole body, his whole life, seemed to tell us, yes, this is possible. Reverend Njoya's response—that of generosity in the face of brutality—so moved his assailants that it was they who rushed him to the hospital where doctors saved him.

Reverend Njoya's ability to re-channel the energy of his fear saved his life.

Anna and I lay awake in our guest house bunks talking a long time that night, and since then I've reflected many times on Rev. Njoya's story. I've learned that I don't have to pray that my fear will—finally, finally—go away and leave me alone. Nor do I have to reach Reverend Njoya's level of self-mastery in order to recognize that, yes, fear is within me, not in an external force. I can harness the energy of fear and, like the lion taking aim, choose where and what I do with it.

FEAR AND CONFLICT

As fear spreads throughout our culture, it's not surprising that many of us are even more tempted to run from conflict—to duck for cover. "In times of danger," writes Rush Dozier in *Fear Itself,* "when there is no immediate avenue of escape, [our brain's] primitive fear system tries to shut off any unnecessary movement, reasoning that if you stay still you might not be noticed."[127]

Not crossing anyone, we stay under the radar, or at least that's the hope of the primitive brain. Imagine the rabbit frozen motionless in the grass.

Willie Manteris, fifty-seven, whom I met in 2003 in an airport coffee shop far from home, told me that, in effect, he'd been that rabbit most of his life. Willie had achieved his dream—a successful dentistry practice in a Pittsburgh suburb, a big home on Club House Drive, two bright children, and a wife with a prestigious job. "In my family growing up, conflict was terrifying, destructive, and upsetting—something to be avoided at all costs," Willie told me, as we sat chatting in Porto Alegre, Brazil. "I had built my whole life by making no waves; conflict was the worst taboo, the worst fear."

But since Willie and I were both on our way home from the World Social Forum, the largest gathering anywhere of citizens trying as hard as they could to make waves, something obviously had changed for Willie.

Three years earlier, Willie had sold his dentistry practice to follow his heart. "The biggest fear and the most powerful was the hidden and invisible one: It was stepping out of the conformity and anonymity, stepping out of old roles in which I felt safe and comfortable. It meant defining the self: who I really was, who I was in the world. It meant risking conflict."

And Willie did, as he began traveling regularly to Central America with Pastors for Peace, offering both material supplies and challenging widespread abuses of indigenous people's rights.

"One of the prices you pay for staying trapped by that fear is that you don't learn how to express healthy dissent. Stepping out of those shadows and voicing oneself is too scary. Politically, it put me for most of my life in a role of being submissive and passive," Willie said.

The consequences of staying stuck in conflict aversion, as Willie had been, are momentous. Fear of conflict too often keeps good people silent, blocking us from participating as the full-voiced citizens of a real democracy we could be.

Even more worrisome, if we fear we can't handle conflict ourselves, we may be tempted to choose authoritarian, "strongman" leaders. In taking us to war in Iraq, I noticed that George W. Bush typically spoke about what "I" the president will do, but rarely about what we as citizens could do—reinforcing feelings of helplessness, the sense that all we can do is put our fate in his hands.

As long as we don't feel we have what it takes to face conflict, do we unconsciously hope authoritarians will squash conflict for us? Burmese Nobel Peace Laureate Aung San Suu Kyi—who, for her pro-democracy heroism, has been brutalized by a military elite, held under house arrest for years, and is still in detention—shares this worry:

"It is not power that corrupts, but fear," Suu Kyi writes in *Freedom from Fear.* "Fear of losing power corrupts those who wield it and fear of the scourge of power corrupts those who are subject to it."[128]

AS IT IS

I believe Aung San Suu Kyi is talking about not just fear of confronting brutal dictators but an even wider fear of standing up to bullying. Mostly, the fear is psychological. Lab studies show that many go along with the majority, even when we *know* the majority is wrong, and all that's at stake is the risk of being out of step. Rather than buck an official-looking authority, more than six out of ten of us, disturbing studies show, will obey even when it means inflicting pain on others.[129]

I love focusing on evidence that positive human qualities enabling us to "live democracy"—including the basic need for fairness and capacity for empathy—are virtually universal. But I also believe the word "virtually" in that sentence needs our attention.

My own life experience and psychiatric experts tell me that, mainly due to being brutalized as youngsters, a tiny minority of us are deficient in empathetic sensibilities—i.e., lack conscience—that almost all of us take for granted. In fact, it's *because* these sensibilities are so widespread that many people have difficulty acknowledging they might be missing in a few.[130] At the extreme, I have witnessed this dysfunction show up in lying without guilt, hurting without remorse, and intimidating with satisfaction.

The want or imperfection of a moral sense in some men, like the want or imperfection of the senses of sight and hearing in others, is no proof that it is a general characteristic of the species.

—THOMAS JEFFERSON, 1814[131]

And why bring up this sad point? The last thing I want to do is heighten the mistrust spread by our dominant culture's frame. But I also know we can't heal our planet unless we perceive life as it is, not as we wish it to be.

I think of what I'm striving for as *heart-centered realism*.

It includes gaining strength to "walk with our fear" of conflict so that we can name harmful dysfunction and rally ourselves and others to effectively contain its damage. Groups taking seriously the notion that democracy is at its root about "how we treat one another" deliberately spell out standards of interaction to which members commit because they've helped choose them. The commitments often include respectful listening and constructive feedback, essential to the democratic arts in Chapter 5.

Making such commitments explicit provides protection: clear bounds the group can enforce, if necessary, so the destructiveness of a tiny minority need not upend the good work of many.[132]

Heart-centered realism means gaining the tools—including rethinking fear—to stand up to bullying, whether within our own house or the White House. It means gaining the confidence to stand up to "group think," as, for example, when in 2002 and early 2003 the Bush White House used false evidence—and bullied those who questioned it—regarding Iraq's threat in order to persuade Americans to back the administration's longstanding intent to invade. Almost all the nation's major media went along—with the striking exception of two Knight Ridder News Service journalists Jonathan Landay and Warren Strobel who dug for the facts and stood by them—despite their admitted queasiness about being out of step.[133]

Our culture doesn't prepare us for such bravery on which Living Democracy depends, but psychologist Martha Stout of the Harvard Medical School offers commonsense advice:

"Trust your own instincts and anxieties, especially those concerning people who claim that dominating others, violence, war, or some other violation of your conscience is the grand solution," she writes. "Do this even when, or especially when, everyone around you has completely stopped questioning authority..." Note that in lab experiments on human complicity in brutality, when even a few people resist, others join them.[134]

Living Democracy demands that we ask ourselves: Even if a tiny minority suffers an empathy deficit, can we in good conscience blame them? Their power to harm is always inversely proportional to the courage exhibited by others who are, after all, the majority. Maybe this realization is what it really means to grow up as a species.

And it means we must rethink fear itself so that we can see what some others may not want to see and say what they may not want to hear.

OLD THOUGHTS, NEW THOUGHTS

It is an extraordinary era: We alive today may be the first in human evolution able to look at how our biology serves us—or does not serve us—and then to choose: We can respond in old, programmed ways—flee, fight, freeze—or we can know fear simply as information. It may well be information that we're pushing our growth edge, with fear's energy now available for creative ends.

We are to learn about fear, not how to escape from it.

—JIDDU KRISHNAMURTI

Instead of robbing us of power, I came to see fear as a resource we use to create the world we want. I've always imagined Reverend Njoya's attackers as seven swordsmen at his door, and now I realize that, like him, we each will meet our seven swordsmen. Only for us, they are our culture's dangerous ideas about fear. *Idea 7* contrasts seven limiting thoughts about fear that I've experienced and seven new, freeing ones.

Each of these ideas frames a chapter in *You Have the Power: Choosing Courage in a Culture of Fear,* which I wrote with Jeffrey Perkins.

I now believe that, like Reverend Njoya, we can transform these assailants into that which can save us.

INNER APPLAUSE

Indeed, the future of life on our beleaguered planet may hinge on such mental jujitsu. Can we learn to transform fear by reinterpreting its meaning? The pounding heart, the tight throat, the weak knees…all may mean we're doing exactly what our truer selves most want in that moment.

Idea 7: Seven Ways to Rethink Fear	
OLD THOUGHTS	**NEW THOUGHTS**
Fear means I'm in danger. Something's wrong. I must escape and seek safety.	Fear is pure energy. It's a signal. It might not mean stop, it could mean go!
If I stop what I'm doing, I'll be lost. I'll never start again.	Sometimes we have to stop in order to find our path.
I have to figure it all out before I can do anything.	We don't have to believe we can do it to do it; the decision to act itself has power.
If I act on what I believe, conflict will break out. I'll be humiliated, ineffective, and rejected.	Conflict means engagement. Something real is in motion. It's an opening, not a closing.
Our greatest fears are our worst enemies; they drag us down and hold us back.	Our worst fears can be our greatest teachers.
If I'm really myself, I'll be excluded. If I break connection, I'll be alone forever.	To find genuine connection, we must risk disconnection. The new light we shine draws others toward us, and we become conscious choosers.
I'm just a drop in the bucket. My effort might make me feel better, but it can't do much.	Every time we act, even with fear, we make room for others to do the same. Courage is contagious.
From *You Have the Power: Choosing Courage in a Culture of Fear* by Frances Moore Lappé and Jeffrey Perkins, Tarcher/Penguin 2004.	

I recall sitting in an audience after Al Gore presented the Boston debut of "An Inconvenient Truth." I was moved by the film; yet I was alarmed, too. Why didn't his prescription for solutions match the magnitude of global climate chaos? Why didn't he emphasize the essential step: removing the power of concentrated wealth from our political decision making?

As soon as the question popped into my head, my heart started to pound. Because other questioners were showering Gore with praise, I realized I'd be out of sync if I were to speak up. Then something new happened. As soon as I became aware of the thump-thump-thump in my chest, I knew I *had* to raise my hand.

My body was telling me something—not that I was a wimp, but that what I had to say was important. That's when I realized I could choose to reinterpret my pounding heart as secret "inner applause" telling me that I'm really exactly where I should be.

By the way, Al Gore never did call on me that night…but I left partially satisfied, anyway, knowing that I didn't shrink back.

So let us expose as myth the notion of "getting over fear." In being true to ourselves, we will always risk separation, and separation will always be frightening. But we can each learn to walk ever taller with our fear, as we lead the way toward life.

9 SANITY IN MOTION

It is far too late and things
are far too bad for pessimism.
—DEE HOCK, FOUNDER OF VISA[135]

Even when a task seems monumental—cleaning out the attic or writing a book—I do find the energy to tackle it *if* I can see first steps. *If* I can see how a small action—getting together a few boxes or creating a one-page outline—connects to my ultimate goal, an attic where I can actually find things, or a book that might help me find answers. I feel overwhelmed until I have an idea of how to get started and a picture of how it will add up to something.

So as we seek to connect our passions with the world's needs in ways that really do add up, my hope for this book is that what I find freeing will also help you:

...that while prevailing assumptions blind us to possibilities for ourselves and our planet, we each can crack open our mental frames to see anew

...that each action we take, *or don't,* makes ripples, so we can with precise intention use our power to reverse causal patterns now spinning our world toward disaster

...that in this historic moment fear needn't stop us, for we can transmute its energy into a source of insight and strength

...and finally, that none of us is alone, nor do we have to start the river flowing. Millions of others in diverse cultures are already inviting us in.

CLAIMING OUR SANITY

I once heard insanity defined as doing the same thing over and over again and expecting it to turn out differently (attributed to both Benjamin Franklin and Albert Einstein but possibly never uttered by either!). I smiled inside...for I have to admit falling prey at times to this grand delusion.

Maybe we all have.

But on the most crucial questions of our time, humanity and the earth itself can no longer survive our refusal to learn.

So I've titled this final chapter "sanity in motion" because that's what's required—that we claim our sanity by probing so deeply that we're able to see the patterns trapping us in this horrific mess. I believe we can stop repeating the "same-olds" and expecting something better to happen. Grasping causal patterns, we can feel excited—not loath—to change.

Let me recount for you, with a few new twists, the realizations I've come to as I've attempted to peel away the layers for my own sanity.

Under its front cover, this little book begins with the dangerously false premise in the center of it all: there isn't *enough*. There aren't enough goods, nor is there enough goodness.

And now some tell us time itself is lacking. We have no time to draw people into solutions-making and build democratic skills and communities; the planet is on the ropes. Top-down strategies are efficient, we still hear, even though they got us into this mess to begin with and suppress precisely the networks of creativity and commitment on which real solutions depend. We have no time for democracy, we're still told, even though it's inconceivable that we can make right our relationship to the earth without making right our relationships with one another.

But the most debilitating piece of the scarcity message is its insistence on lack inside us. A tawdry self-concept drives the dominant worldview. This shrunken view of our essence is reinforced not only by dominant political and economic theory, not only by incessant corporate advertising, but also by strains within many of the world's religions. The first two reduce us to competitive accumulators; the third may be even worse—emphasizing that we're unclean sinners.

From this premise of lack, we *are* finished. We end up locked in a belief system that actually creates the very scarcity we fear.

With this dim view of ourselves, we're vulnerable to simplistic social dogma—to grand "isms"—encouraging us to turn over our fate to infallible laws, like the mythical "free market" and to distant institutions, such as the formal trappings of democracy, not to mention dictators and ayatollahs.

Here in the West, where market dogma has many spellbound, we allow a one-rule economy to take hold (economic life driven by highest return to existing wealth) that inevitably concentrates money and decision making in the hands of a tiny minority. This concentration kills precisely what we say we hold quite dear—a competitive market and political decision making accountable to the public good.

Our planet's survival therefore depends on whether we can make the break—whether we can affirm not, as I've stressed, the goodness *of* human nature but the richness *in* human nature.

Nature, it turns out, has equipped us with just what we need to make this great turning: our hard-wired needs and capacities for community bonding, for meaning and efficacy beyond day-to-day survival, and for fairness. We are also profoundly creative, learning creatures. "Fortunately, the human brain comes equipped with a very special feature," writes radiology and psychiatry professor Andrew Newberg. "It can alter its system of beliefs far more rapidly than that of any other organism on the planet."

The challenge is to believe that a new, more life-serving world view is—at least possibly—emerging. "Seeing is believing" is a charming aphorism, but maybe it's also wrong. More accurately, when it comes to humans, "believing is seeing." We must believe another way of living is possible in order to see it actually taking shape around us.

Maybe, though, the only way to see the new is to become part of the new.

As my daughter Anna and I traveled the world to write *Hope's*

Edge, we observed that the most hopeful people, those with the greatest sense of possibility, were hardly the most advantaged. But what they did have in common was easy to spot: they were taking the biggest risks; they were engaged, heart and soul.

Hope is not what we find in evidence.
It is what we become in action.

—MOTTO OF THE SMALL PLANET INSTITUTE

PROTECTION

But to take part in the birth of the new also requires, as I noted in this book's opening pages, that we let go of a central, ego-satisfying myth. For eons, humans have pointed fingers at the evil "other," claiming themselves to be incapable of the inhumanity of the perpetrator. So the task was clear: Rid the world of the evildoer! But at the dawn of the twenty-first century, evidence defies this simple, ego-salving prescription. Once we admit the Holocaust, Rwanda, Hiroshima, and so much more, humanity can face the truth that these are horrific acts by "normal people" inflicting suffering and death on innocents.

Understandably, human beings have resisted this painful admission. But actually, there is reward in finding the courage to face it. Freed from the idea that our misery is caused by an incurably evil "other," we are able to ask: *Okay, what exactly are the conditions under which brutality will almost certainly surface?* If we can identify with some confidence the conditions that bring out the worst in us, we can address them.

Social psychologists and cultural historians tell us that the conditions are not so difficult to discern.[136] Among them are:

- extreme imbalances in power that thwart the creative energies of the disempowered and distort the humanity of the powerful.
- anonymity that shields us from accountability and distances us from our innate connection and caring.
- negative labeling that dehumanizes others and leads to their being scapegoated.
- the grip of absolutist ideologies that teach us to distrust our own common sense.

Clarity gives us power to create the world we want. It enables us to choose Living Democracy, knowing that its qualities, values, and practices sketched through this book help us to uproot *each* of these four abuse-generating conditions. As we make democracy a way of life, we:

- continually disperse power by building decision-making structures of mutual accountability and by nurturing the skills to hold accountable those in positions of greater authority.
- dissolve anonymity by enhancing community bonds and transparency.
- lessen the likelihood of stereotyping and demonizing others by linking diverse people and building communication skills.
- and finally, because ongoing learning is at the heart of Living

Democracy, we replace absolutist thinking with creativity.
It follows that as we learn to live democracy we can protect ourselves from the worst in us so that we can manifest the best.

And how to begin?

A CAUTIONARY TALE, THE DANGER OF GOOD INTENTIONS

Before answering directly, let me share a cautionary tale from the 1970s. Joe Collins and I, both barely thirty years old, had just met through our common outrage over world hunger, which for the first time had hit the international marquee. We were determined to create an institute (ultimately, becoming the Institute for Food and Development Policy, a.k.a. Food First) with a strong voice helping to find solutions.

We heard most public voices, especially those within religious communities, calling for food aid—shipping our food at low or no cost to hungry nations—as the moral response: We have so much and they have so little, so let's transfer some of our bounteous supply to them. American farmers felt heroic as they responded to the call.

On the surface, who could argue? The simple logic moved hearts.

But Joe and I, burying ourselves in research about the hungriest places on earth, learned startling facts: Many of these nations produced enough for all to eat, only many of their people were too poor to buy it. And much potential production was untapped. Moreover, we discovered that chronically importing subsidized food can undercut local farmers, depriving them of markets, and shift tastes away from locally grown foods—both making future food self-reliance more difficult.

Yes, providing short-term food aid to poor countries is absolutely essential to save lives in emergencies, but food in most cases can be bought within the region, thus benefiting poor farmers nearby. Operating within Thin Democracy, U.S. agribusiness has been able to block this commonsense approach and cause deadly delays in famine relief by insisting our government use only U.S. suppliers.[137]

So "food aid" became my own personal code words for, "Good intentions aren't enough. They can even backfire!"

ON ISSUES VERSUS ENTRY POINTS

To avoid the unintended backfiring of "helpful" acts, we can dig to root causes, always asking: How am I interrupting a negative cycle that creates suffering or reinforcing a positive one that contributes to new, life-serving rules and norms?

To answer that question, for me it's helpful to distinguish between "issues" and "entry points."

"Issues" overwhelm. They hit us as distinct problems, piles and piles of them. We hear of child slavery, violence against women, hunger, of HIV/AIDS, deepening inequality, pollution and global heating, depression, failing schools…

I feel buried, smothered under a mountain of problems. I want to cry uncle.

"Entry points" are very different.

Entry points we can detect because we're weaving a theory of causation. So we can pinpoint places to start to shift the killer cycle itself. On the surface they might appear as distinct problems, but they are ways "in": They are sharp points that break into and deflect the *Spiral of Powerlessness* presented inside the front cover. They are deliberate actions that strengthen the flow of causation, putting in motion the *Spiral of Empowerment* presented inside the back cover.

To make these distinctions clearer, let me compare five issues with five entry points.

Entry point 1: removing money's grip on democracy

An "issue" is the need to elect a courageous candidate for office who "gets it." But since a major cause of thinning democracy is the power of money over political decision making, for me, an entry point is removing that power.

So let me introduce you to Marge Mead of Sun City, Arizona.

Marge, seventy-seven, a mother of eight with ten grandchildren, took her first college class when she was forty-two and got her master's degree at fifty-one. After years of teaching, "I was tired of correcting freshman compositions," she told us, "so I retired, and my husband and I moved here." She felt like a fish out of water until she attended a meeting of the Sun City Democratic Club. Soon Marge became a precinct and state committee person. She joined the League of Women Voters.

In 1996, several League leaders were going to be away for the summer, and Marge was asked to fill in at meetings to shape a law to clean up campaigns. "I was pretty ignorant about details of the law," Marge said, "and ignorant about politics in general."

But she felt strongly about money's corrupting power. She summed up the problem this way: "Big campaign donors aren't in it for altruism. They don't consider their money a contribution; they consider it an investment." (And a pretty sound one, too.)

So Marge went to the campaign finance reform meeting as a stand-in. The goal was "Clean Elections" in Arizona, a voluntary system of public finance. (Candidates hoping to receive public funds must collect a certain number of small "qualifying contributions" from registered voters. Then the candidate takes no private money, and the government provides a fixed sum for campaigning. If Clean Elections candidates are outspent by privately funded opponents, they may get additional public matching funds.)

"I walked in and said, 'Who's taking notes?' 'Well, we're all taking notes here and there.' And I said, 'You should have someone taking minutes because this is a historic happening. And you can't remember all the nuances of discussions.' So they asked, 'Will you take the notes?' Being an old secretary, I knew shorthand and typed quite well. So I became the secretary."

Marge's insistence on having formal minutes may be the act that launched what she called her "latest incarnation, that of political activist"—a citizen leader in a critical battle for democracy.

"I was in awe," she told us. "It was a new concept and rather radical. I was amazed at the dedication of other members of the coalition.

"At first, I felt insecure; the law is complicated. But I traveled all over the place talking to various groups. I went to Glendale Community College, where I had been an instructor, and talked to social studies classes. It was exhilarating, and I became increasingly confident."

To bring the Clean Elections Act to a vote, the coalition had to collect 10 percent of the number of votes cast for governor in the previous election—that was 112,961 signatures. "And when it came to the vote, we [voluntary public financing] squeaked by with 51 percent," Marge said.

The law took effect in 1998. Predictably, wealthy narrow-interest groups, accustomed to buying the attention of politicians, have battled Clean Elections every step of the way. In Arizona, bankers, developers, and corporate lobbyists—calling themselves No Taxpayer Money for Politicians—spent half a million dollars trying to get a dubiously worded question on the 2004 ballot to kill Clean Elections.

They failed.

Clean Elections didn't start in Arizona with grandma Marge and her League buddies, though. Maine came first in 1996, when twenty-six-year-old political science grad David Donnelly led the reform. Today about 80 percent of Maine's legislators have "run clean." Without Clean Elections "I wouldn't have dared to try," says Mainer Deb Simpson, forty-five, who was a waitress and single mom when elected to the state legislature in 2000. She now co-chairs the judiciary committee. Armed with proof that the approach draws candidates and voters in and keeps money out, citizens in fifteen states are crafting similar laws.

Entry point 2: empowering kids

An "issue" is kids failing in school and getting into trouble with the law, especially poor kids. But probing more deeply to find an entry point, we realize that beneath that failure are feelings of powerlessness, hopelessness, and lack of self-valuing.

That's the entry point my hero Edgar Cahn saw.

Twenty-five years ago, law school professor Edgar found himself in an intensive care unit recovering from a major heart attack, suddenly reliant on others. He felt useless and started to wonder about other so-called throwaway people—the elderly, the young, the sick, the poor. He imagined that many felt like he did. They didn't want to be treated like helpless victims, and they hungered to contribute.

A lean and serious man, Edgar, now seventy, invented an elegantly simple tool, a tax-exempt "currency" not for buying more stuff but a currency we could use to get help we might need; and "earn by helping others." He called it "Time Dollars," whereby one hour of service provided earns oneself one hour of service in return—be it a lift to the doctor's, a leaky pipe fixed, a hot meal prepared, or a tutoring session. You earn Time Dollars for each service you perform and then spend it on whatever you want from listings in an online Time Bank. The key for Edgar is that all services are afforded equal value.

In Washington, D.C., Edgar used the Time Dollar deal when he founded Teen Courts, in which peers judge nonviolent youth offenders. Serving on a jury, ex-offenders earn Time Dollars that they can then use to buy a recycled computer. Among the one-quarter of youth offenders in Washington, D.C., who have been assigned to such courts, only 15 to 17 percent get into trouble again, a fraction of the typical rate of re-offense.[138] Imagine the revolutionary potential of the youth court in a city where more than half of all young black men aged eighteen to twenty-four are under court jurisdiction.

Edgar's approach is alive in schools, too. Believing that the need to give is as deep for kids as for adults, he told Chicago school authorities "Find us any fifth and sixth graders willing to put in about a hundred hours tutoring younger kids and earn a recycled computer. The schools sent us the special education kids and those with attention deficit problems," Edgar said.

As students went from being "underachievers" to becoming mentors, attendance went up on tutoring days, and fighting after school stopped—"tutors didn't let anyone beat up their tutees," Edgar noted.

And then there's YouthBuild.

In 1978, a former Harlem elementary school teacher in her thirties, Dorothy Stoneman, wanted to do her part to uproot the racism and poverty hurting her students. Realizing the power of young people themselves, she asked East Harlem teenagers a straightforward question, "What would you do to improve your community if you had adult support?"

"We'd rebuild the houses. We'd take empty buildings back from the drug dealers and eliminate crime," they told her. Together, they and Dorothy formed what became YouthBuild to renovate a tenement building.

Since then, sixty-eight thousand young people, living in poor communities and previously unable to see a future, have through

YouthBuild produced sixteen thousand units of affordable housing, earned their GED, apprenticed in the building trades, and learned the arts of democracy.

YouthBuilders experience themselves not as recipients of help but as powerful contributors, says Dorothy (who, I am happy to say, is now my friend). Besides their construction achievements, they also help choose staff, raise funds, and share in leading the national organization.

The movement has spread to two hundred twenty-six sites reaching almost all states and now is being called to other countries, starting with South Africa and Mexico. Graduates tell Dorothy that "without YouthBuild, I would probably be dead or in jail. Instead I am building homes, going to college, and making a difference."

"YouthBuild graduates don't just have tools helping *them* live better," says Dorothy. "They've become citizens and leaders making the world better for us all."

Entry point 3: power shopping

Which head of lettuce you pick up today or where you buy your next T-shirt may not seem like a world-changing decision. But it is.

The *Spiral of Powerlessness* is generated not only by laws on the books but by norms that our daily acts create. If we buy pesticide-sprayed food, we're saying to the food industry, yes, yes, give me more of that. If we buy organic instead, we are stimulating its production. (Why do you think McDonald's serves organic milk in Sweden but not here?) True, these marketplace "votes" are grossly lopsided—for the more money one has, the more votes one gets—but our purchases make ripples nonetheless.

I say this not to make us feel guilty but to help us realize our power.

Sixty-three million Americans now say they base their purchasing decisions on how they affect the world, and four out of five say they're likely to switch brands to help support a cause when price and quality are equal.

Even ten years ago this was hardly the case. Why the change? Perhaps it's that we're learning to see what's been invisible. We can now readily calculate the environmental impact of our daily choices at, for example, myfootprint.org.

And other new on-line tools are popping up. CoopAmerica offers on-line its National Green Pages guide to environmentally sound businesses.[139] Another tool is Alonovo.com, which reminds us that "every time we make a purchase we are transferring power to a business." The site rates hundreds of products on several counts—from social responsibility and the environment to a fair workplace and the producer's ethics.

Worldwide, sales in the Fair Trade movement, I noted in Chapter 2, jumped by over 50 percent in just one year, 2004. It now functions in fifty countries because millions of consumers are seeking out its label, guaranteeing that producers receive a decent return. Just to take one example of its impact: In 2006, Rwandan coffee cooperatives whose members include widows and orphans of the 1994 genocide, received a Fair Trade price for their coffee three times what local merchants offered.

This sea change in awakening to the power of our purchasing choices comes to us also thanks to some energetic, determined people. One is Lina Musayev. Now twenty-five, Lina was a student at George Washington University when her life changed forever during a 2002 Oxfam America leadership training intensive.

"Farmers from Guatemala came to talk to us," Lina told me. "We got the real story of Fair Trade from the roots. I didn't know anything about the coffee crisis. I didn't know it affected twenty-five million people. So when I heard about Fair Trade, I thought, 'This is incredible. It's working. It's making a difference.'

"The next day, literally, my friend Stephanie [Faith Green], who'd come with me from Georgetown University, and I founded United Students for Fair Trade.

"She and I are really close. We made a great team.

"Once school started, I decided to start from the bottom with a petition saying students wanted more Fair Trade coffee, and we got two thousand students to sign. That's out of ten thousand. It worked. We sent a letter to Starbucks. We pushed for Fair Trade coffee at every university event, like teachers' meetings."

I asked Lina what approach she'd found most effective in reaching students.

"The main thing is getting farmers themselves to come to the campus. Hearing the farmers, I see the students say, 'Oh, my gosh—I didn't know this.' Almost like I was!"

After three years, George Washington passed a resolution that called on all on-campus vending outlets to serve 100 percent Fair Trade coffee. In only five years, the student Fair Trade movement Lina and her friend Stephanie launched has spread to three hundred campuses, and roughly fifty campuses now serve only Fair Trade coffee.

Lina and Stephanie would probably find it hard ever again to view economics as simply about things exchanged in anonymous transactions. They are helping shape a new norm, an economy that's about people, people relating with each other—fairly.

Entry point 4: citizen to producer: "you made it, you're responsible"

An "issue" is mountains of electronic waste, much of it toxic, clogging landfills, as well as the planet-heating burning of fossil fuels used to manufacture millions of new electronic gadgets every year—in part because so few get recycled.

Making a PC monitor, it turns out, uses ten times its weight in fossil fuels, while cars and refrigerators use between one and two times their weight. So the annual manufacturing of 130 million computers contributes both to the spread of toxic chemicals and to global heating.

One way to confront this issue would be to make stricter rules about what consumers must do with obsolete electronics.

But…an *entry point*?

An entry point shifts the inner logic of the problem. And that's what Maine citizens began in early 2006 when their new "producer responsibility" law went into effect: It requires producers putting certain electronic products into our world also to carry responsibility for their life cycle, including the cost of recycling.

Suddenly, with that one shift, producers are motivated to make less toxic and more recyclable things.

"It's too wasteful to try to retrofit after things are built. We don't have time. We have to build sustainability into products," Pete Didisheim, advocacy director for the Natural Resources Council of Maine, which led a campaign making Maine the first U.S. state to enact "producer responsibility." The approach is big in Europe and on the books now in twenty-nine countries.

The producer-responsibility fire in Pete's belly got lit a few years ago when he watched a shocking video, *Exporting Harm*. He saw unprotected workers in China dismantling discarded computers from the industrial countries and unknowingly exposing themselves to deadly lead, cadmium, and other toxics.

"This is the dark side of our information age," he told me.

So he, along with the Maine environmental council, got busy and found legislative sponsors (including a Republican landfill operator who had seen the problem close up) to introduce a bill to get to the root of the crisis.

Before the bill, each year Mainers threw out an estimated one hundred thousand computers and televisions, each with an array of toxic materials inside, including deadly mercury and three to eight pounds of toxic lead. Because much waste in Maine is incinerated, a lot of harmful fumes were polluting this breathtaking state.

Now, manufacturers pick up most of the cost of dismantling and recycling TVs and computer monitors. Consumers are required to take televisions and monitors to a transfer station; from there they go to state-approved centers that recycle them and bill manufacturers for the cost—as much as forty-eight cents a pound.

"It was an uphill battle," Pete said. Industry lobbyists mounted the biggest effort ever in this state. But because of the Clean Elections law, they couldn't "sprinkle campaign checks across the State House to help kill the bill. All the big computer makers—IBM, Panasonic, Mitsubishi…did put tens of millions into TV and print ads opposing it. Apple, despite its progressive image, was the worst. Only Hewlett-Packard supported the bill. It sees recovery of used computers as a business opportunity."

"Producer responsibility" sends major ripples back through the electronics industry, including designing more long-lasting, more easily recyclable, and less toxic products and less fossil fuel use because recycling means less manufacturing from scratch.

Just five months into the new system, Mainers had already saved from the waste stream almost a million pounds of TVs and over a third of a million pounds of monitors.

An even more vigorous law passed in 2006 in Washington, and similar bills have been introduced in a half dozen states.

Entry point 5: reward "renewables"

Finally, an urgent "issue" is global heating, the danger of nuclear power, and the need for non-polluting, non-planet-heating, safe, renewable energy sources.

But where's the entry point in a global economy dominated by a trillion-dollar-plus oil industry?

Many people devoting their lives to getting us off fossil fuel say one pretty simple policy instrument stands out. Speeding deployment of renewable energy technologies in over forty-one countries, states, and provinces is what's called the "feed-in tariff," with the great acronym, FIT. Germany and Spain are leading the way.

The law simply obligates utilities to buy electricity from renewable installations at a price carefully calculated to ensure profits from the new sources. Green energy producers are thus guaranteed a good market, and investment risk is virtually zero. Even householders who produce electricity from wind or solar are invited in on the act. As billions in public subsidies now go to benefit the fossil fuel and nuclear industries, feed-in laws begin to correct the grossly tilted playing field.

In Germany, costs are spread among all bill-paying households, so the law adds only around €1.50 ($2.00) a month for each.

In southern Germany, the seven hundred people of the village of Jühnde demonstrate the law's potential. All its energy, 100 percent, now comes from renewable sources, including farm wastes, according to Miguel Mendonca, author of the first definitive book on the subject, *Feed-in Tariffs*.[140]

In Spain, Miguel told me of big "solar parks" an hour's drive from Pamplona, next to a village called Milagro: "They have one of Europe's biggest—the size of fifty football pitches [soccer fields]—with arrays of huge solar photovoltaic panels. The solar park is run cooperatively—as are more and more such installations—with around seven hundred fifty owners. A tax break reduces the investment cost per panel, and the feed-in tariff brings a guaranteed annual income. As a result, there are plenty of enthusiastic investors."

Milagro's mayor Esteban Garijo thinks it is a brilliant idea: "On sunny days, the sun doesn't cost us anything. So not only are we generating clean energy, but the town is making money."

In nearby Navarra, some local residents now invest in solar panels to generate funds for retirement.

Unbelievable as it might seem, a 1999 feed-in type law signed by then Governor George W. Bush has made Texas into America's wind energy champion. In 2005, Washington State joined the club, and citizens in Wisconsin are campaigning heavily for it.

A barrier to renewables, writes Miguel, is the myth that they can provide only a small share of our energy. Wrong, he says. "If the world's fossil and nuclear fuels were to disappear tomorrow, you can bet that renewables would quite quickly" do the job.[141] And for motivation to act now, note that polluting coal plants are still being built world wide at the pace of one a week.

In sum, Clean Elections is an entry point because the strategy breaks the grip of money over governance. Time Dollars, teen courts, and YouthBuild are entry points because they interrupt the downward *Spiral of Powerlessness*, illustrated inside the front cover, by positively remaking the false views of ourselves that lie at the very heart of Thin Democracy.

Power shopping and Fair Trade, as well as producer-responsibility and feed-in laws—like other strategies to integrate corporations into the ecology of democracy—also reverse the negative spiral because we learn that the market is not an infallible law beyond our reach. It is a tool we can use consciously to manifest our values. That's the confidence we need to fuel the *Spiral of Empowerment* creating a world calling out the best in us.

AN INTERNAL CHECKLIST

Joyful living, I'm convinced, happens when we hit that spot where a potent entry point that touches root causes fires our own deep passions. I know that when I first discovered that spot—my mid-twenties' "aha" that our daily eating habits make huge ecological and fairness ripples—it set off a personal revolution, and I've been forever grateful.

To find that spot, a critical first step may be to recognize that the negative spiral can start deep inside us. If a feeling of "lack" lurks at the center of our pain, pain that we then project out and create in the world, we can start within ourselves to reverse it: We can acknowledge sufficiency. Right now, we can focus on the strengths of ourselves and our loved ones and the possibilities in front of our noses to enhance our capacities and meet our needs for fairness, cooperation, efficacy, and meaning.

Awareness of these capacities can propel the spiral of empowerment busting us out of any downward spin.

So think of something you are doing right now. Maybe you are engaged in your children's schools to make them more empowering for students, or you're sending off an email to the newspaper shaping your community's views. (Remember that even if it's not printed, someone has read it and registered a reader's concerns.)

Maybe you just became a supporter of community radio, or you are exploring whether your congregation might join the three million Americans working for basic fairness in our society through their faith communities.

Maybe you've chosen to lighten your weight on the planet by eating less meat, converting your home to solar energy, or joining in "community-supported agriculture" by buying a share in a nearby farm's produce. Maybe you are finally speaking about discrimination you see in your workplace or going door-to-door on behalf of a candidate who is actually listening to citizens' concerns.

Then think about what you've always wanted to do.

In each case, you might pose questions to yourself about your choices and dreams. In finding my own way, a core question for me has become, *How do I know Living Democracy when I see it?* I want a checklist in my head to help me make choices, so I've developed *Idea 8*, Living Democracy's Checklist organized around five big questions. They help me weigh whether a given approach is interrupting the destructive causal flow and speeding the life-enhancing *Spiral of Empowerment.*

I hope these questions help you, too. Add your own, of course, and as you try it out, please visit smallplanetinstitute.org. This book is built in part on *Hope's Edge* and *Democracy's Edge*, which are full of dozens and dozens of entry points to help readers connect their passions with deep change. Read, talk with others. Wander a bit, too, and see what fires you up.

BOLD HUMILITY

At a party I threw in the 1970s, I recall the line of a comedian friend who cracked everyone up: "Yeah…I once considered going into Lappé's line of work—trying to change the world," he said, deadpan, "but one problem stopped me. You know, you can go for *weeks* and not see any change at all!"

Yes, we all laughed, but I realize now my funny friend might have missed the *real* challenge.

Back then I never could have imagined the world as I experience it today: I assumed things would get better (if people listened to me, of course!); or they would get worse. But, it hasn't turned out that way. Things are moving fast in two directions at once: they are getting very much worse *and* they are getting very much better. The real challenge is staying sane in this both/and world: it is holding both realities.

Helping me is a new kind of humility taking root inside. I can now look at all the positive developments emerging and admit I would have given them almost zero probability of success when I was my children's age. That's humbling.

I realize also that most of the Living Democracy initiatives you've encountered in this book began with one person or a small handful of people, and many breakthroughs that most inspire me mark their birth little more than thirty years ago. Plenty are more recent. In historical time, this is no time at all. The rapidity of their growth, the parallels in the lessons being learned, suggests that we would be naïve—just plain silly—to underestimate their potential.

Idea 8: Living Democracy's Checklist
as we probe deeply, identify causal patterns & choose entry points

1. AM I EXPANDING AND SPREADING POWER?
- Does my action create new power—greater awareness and strengthening of my own and others' capacities? Does it reduce power imbalances?
- Is my effort contributing to a one-time correction, or does it generate ongoing, fairer, and more effective decision making?
- Does accountability flow one-way, or are multiple parties taking responsibility and being held accountable?

2. AM I EASING FEAR OF CHANGE AND FEAR OF THE OTHER?
- Am I modeling that it's okay to be afraid as we face the new?
- Does my effort replace stereotyping with valuing and welcoming diversity?
- Am I helping to build group bonds that strengthen courage without excluding others?

3. AM I LEARNING AND TEACHING THE ARTS OF DEMOCRACY?
- Does my effort teach and practice active listening, the creative use of conflict, ongoing evaluation, mentoring, and other essential skills for effectiveness?

4. AM I CREATING MOVEMENT THAT IS SUSTAINABLE?
- Is the initiative made inherently rewarding with big doses of real learning, humor, beauty, celebration, and camaraderie?
- Is it being made widely visible so that those beyond the inner circle are motivated to act? (Don't forget our mirror neurons!)

5. AM I REPLACING THE LIMITING FRAME WITH AN EMPOWERING ONE?
- Am I helping to replace the core presumption of "lack" with that of "plenty"?
- Am I helping to replace belief in fixed economic laws with confidence in human creativity?
- Am I refocusing us on the goodness "in" human nature—our needs for connection, fairness, and effectiveness—we can tap to heal our beautiful planet?

All this makes me think twice about any verdict on the future.

It is not possible to know what's possible, I noted early in this book. This is how I now understand humility. Believing we can accurately predict outcomes, as cynics claim to, has become for me the utmost in hubris. And because this is true, we are free. We are free to act assuming that our action—no matter how small it appears to us—could be the tipping point setting off tectonic shifts of consciousness and creativity.

KNOWING

We cannot predict outcomes, but some things are coming clear: and that clarity is beginning to rattle us: The shock of melting ice caps and dying penguins, of leveled rainforests and species wiped out daily before we've even met them, of children armed in genocidal war, and children dying of hunger even as we feed over a third of all grain to livestock…all of this is sinking in, and more and more of us know the time is now—that we act powerfully now or we see our fate sealed: We risk becoming our species' most shameful ancestors, passing on to those we love and those they will love a diminished world that we ourselves find heartbreaking.

Such shock may then open us to a surge of energy lying dormant—a pure, protective rage we can transform into exuberant defense of our beautiful earth under siege.

Yes, there is much we do not and perhaps cannot know about our chances of success. But there is much we *can* know:

Humanity is coming to understand nature's fundamental laws and the fatal consequences of ignoring them. Rather than triggering panic, our coming to accept nature's boundaries may bring huge relief. If children need boundaries to feel safe, maybe we'll find we all do. Nature offers us real, non-arbitrary guidelines, and as we align ourselves with her—because we ourselves are part of nature—we may also move into greater alignment with one another. Could this shift, truly trusting nature's laws, ultimately release the grip of self-created scarcity, allowing us to experience real abundance for the first time?

Many are also coming to know that just as we need not fight the natural world, we need not fight our own nature. We can trust our deep, in-born needs to "connect and affect." We can trust our ability to walk with fear. We can even trust our capacity to let go of long-held ways of seeing in order to structure our societies to protect us from the worst in us while releasing the best: for we know in our bones that the real problems facing our planet can only be met by the ingenuity, experience, and buy-in—the contagious engagement—of billions of us. Knowing all this, it is at least possible that we can take the biggest leap, embracing the open and dynamic frame that Living Democracy offers us.

So on this exhilarating walk, you'll understand why I love to carry with me the words of friend and acclaimed nature photographer Harold Feinstein. Harold spends his days focused—literally and close-up—on the beauty of plants. In a conversation recently about whether humanity would make it, Harold just grinned:

"Remember," he said, "life loves life. We've got nature on our side."

AN INVITATION

Thank you for engaging with these ideas. We at the Small Planet Institute invite you to use our web site, smallplanetinstitute.org, as a tool to continue to make sense of the world in a way that strengthens you and spurs you on.

Please find there a *Getting a Grip* section where you can join in the conversation. In a user-welcoming format, you'll also find the book's endnotes (with all the many web links) where we invite you to contribute corrections, updates, and suggestions for further exploration.

In 2000, in Kenya, my daughter Anna Lappé and I visited a Green Belt Movement village of women tree planters who are fighting both the encroaching desert and abusive authorities. On the movement's white t-shirts were these seven words: "As for me, I've made a choice."

Their words still stir me, for making a choice to do something—for ourselves, our loved ones, our planet—is an act of courage in a world that teaches us to run from risk. Next you'll find a guide—designed for group or personal reflection—to help transform the ideas you've encountered here into choices in our lives.

QUESTIONS TO SPARK TALK AND ACTION

CHAPTER 1: THE STRAIGHTJACKET

As a whole group, ask:

- When you hear the word "democracy," what first comes to mind?
  Record responses, then discuss what they reveal about the nature of democracy today.

- Do you agree that our mental "frames" largely determine our realities? What examples come to mind?

As a whole group, silently reflect on the *Spiral of Powerlessness* inside the front cover. Then break into twos or threes to discuss:

- How would you adjust this picture to match your own sense of the unspoken assumptions driving our society and their consequences?

Reconvene the group and share insights. Then probe this question:

- How does Lappé's framing of root causes differ from those widely accepted in our society today, especially by liberals and progressives? Consider, for example, the view that the Far Right is to blame, or Jeffrey Sachs' (*The End of Poverty*) view that the problem is poor people abroad being left out of the West's proven, successful economic model.

Activity before next group talk:

- Seek news items that reflect your understanding of the crisis of Thin Democracy and prepare to share them.

CHAPTER 2: NEW EYES

As a whole group, share news items gathered since the first meeting. Then silently review the *Spiral of Empowerment* inside the back cover, starting from the premise of "plenty."

Break into twos or threes to ask:

- Does this spiral of beliefs and their consequences reflect your experience of the world? Explore how you would you alter it to reflect your understanding of a positive cycle leading to greater and greater well-being.

- What do you think Lappé means by "plenty" (since if the world's people emulated U.S. resource use, we'd need a few more planets)? As you mull over this positive spiral, return to the *Spiral of Powerlessness* to compare the two spirals, which start with opposite premises.

Reconvene the group and share insights from the smaller groups. Then silently review *Idea 1: Thin Democracy vs. Living Democracy* and ask:

- Did you grow up absorbing the Thin Democracy definition of democracy? What were the messages about what democracy expected of you?
- Lappé sees Living Democracy emerging as five qualities permeating a culture. What does she mean that the transition to Living Democracy is moving from a focus on fixed institutions to a focus on dynamic relationships reflecting these values? What is missing, and what would you change?

Activity before next session:

- Bring a story of Living Democracy you've experienced or learned about, and be ready to share qualities you find in it that reflect Living Democracy.

CHAPTER 3: WHAT DEMOCRACY FEELS LIKE

As a whole group, share stories of Living Democracy you've experienced or read about.

Then in twos or threes, discuss:

- What stories in this chapter were most surprising and interesting to you? Which do you think are most important in shifting our culture toward health?
- What makes these initiatives effective? How do they jibe, or not, with the defining qualities of Living Democracy highlighted in the Chapter 2?

Reconvene the group for conversation:

- Discuss which dimensions of Living Democracy mentioned in this chapter are already underway in your community and which might be most likely to take root.
- Consider the four "winds in the sails" of Living Democracy the author mentions. Then brainstorm together: What big changes does she fail to mention that make possible the continuing emergence of Living Democracy?

Activity before next group talk:

- Ask friends and family to tell you the first words that come to mind when you say "power." Consider sources of power in your own life.

CHAPTER 4: POWER INVISIBLE

As a whole group, silently review *Idea 3: Rethinking Power*. Then respond:

- What responses did you get when asking others to react to the word "power"?
- Do you share the negative associations with power Lappé says are common? Why or why not? Do you agree that they can limit us?

Then in twos or threes, explore one or both of the following:

- Encourage one another to tell about a moment in life in community when you have felt especially powerful. Why? What enabled these feelings of efficacy?
- Ask one another to identify one assumption about the limits of her or his power. Ask: How might you recast this limit to free you to realize your power?

Reconvene the group to share highlights from the small groups, and if time permits, respond to the question:

- What are examples of contemporary social initiatives you care about—from those in your community to the global level? How do they, or how do they not, build relational power?

Activity before next group talk:

- Look for examples in the news that clarify, challenge, or deepen your view of power and ways to enhance one's own power.

CHAPTER 5: THE ART OF POWER

As a whole group, silently review *Idea 4: Ten Arts of Democracy.* Then consider together:

- Which of these arts do you find most challenging? Why?
- Share stories of individuals using these arts effectively.
- Which art(s) do you most want to hone to use with your family or in your workplace or other associations?

In twos or threes, according to which arts interest participants, ask each to:

- Reflect on opportunities you have right now in your life to consciously develop one or two arts of democracy. Share your hunches about the rewards you would gain by improving these skills.
- Identify one first step you want to take, and consider a partner who might want to pursue the goal with you.
- Reconvene the group to share highlights of small group discussion.

Activities before next session:

- Pick one art you would like especially to hone, and reflect on how you practice it. Use the guide, *Doing Democracy, Ten Practical Arts*, downloadable at www.democracysedge.org/handbook.pdf for suggestions.
- One or more participants may want to volunteer to review the *Doing Democracy* guide and bring back stories and lessons to the next discussion.

CHAPTER 6: TALKING DEMOCRACY

As a whole group, invite those who perused *Doing Democracy: Ten Practical Arts* to share what struck them as most useful.

Before reviewing *Idea 5: Toward a Language of Democracy*, ask one person to read only the words in the left column. As they are read, participants call out the first words or phrases that come to mind. One person records these uncensored responses.

Then as a group, discuss:

- What are the implications of these commonly used words? What associations do participants have with them? How do they shape our thinking without our conscious awareness?

Reconvene the group, silently review *Idea 5*, and discuss:

- Do you agree with Lappé's argument for the importance of consciously choosing new terms?
- Which common terms related to social problem solving—these or others—do you find most blocking dialogue and understanding?

In twos or threes,

- Brainstorm terms you find most problematic and alternatives. Take notes to share with the larger group.
- Choose one or more terms to try out on friends before the next gathering.
- Reconvene the group to share alternative words and reflections on the power of language.

Activities before next session:

- Test out new selected terms before next session.
- Bring to your next session an example of language in the media that disempowers.
- Write letters to a newsmaker/commentator who has used disempowering language, and share your letter with the group.

CHAPTER 7: SEIZE THE MOMENT

As a whole group, review *Idea 6: The Inner World of Living Democracy* in silence.

- Does the downward spiral of fear ring true? Have you experienced yourself or others in such a negative cycle?
- Does the upward spiral ring true? What does Lappé mean by "embrace new tribes"? And how is this possible without getting stuck in new forms of "group-think"?

In twos or threes, explore the following:

- Share moments of dissonance in your lives and the choices you've made in their wake.
- Discuss what the discovery of "mirror neurons" might mean for using these moments of dissonance to move from the "stuckness" of fear's grip to the embrace of new life.

As a whole group, explore:

- Very practically, what do we need to make it more likely that you, and those close to you, can move from the spiral of fear to the spiral of hope?

Activity before next meeting:

- Discuss with loved ones moments of dissonance in our lives and theirs and where these feelings have led us.
- Incorporate into your news intake one new source of connection to positive developments and courageous action.

CHAPTER 8: WHEN FEAR MEANS GO

As a whole group, silently review *Idea 7: Seven Ways to Rethink Fear.*

In twos or threes, consider the seven old thoughts/new thoughts, exploring:

- Why does Lappé argue that how we respond to fear may be the most critical choice in our lives? Explore why you agree or disagree.
- Which of the seven thoughts most resonate in your life experience? Share stories that these thoughts cause to surface.
- Do you feel you can learn to rethink fear as a signal, not a verdict? What difference would this shift make in your life now?

Reconvene the group to discuss:

- How is fear being manipulated for political and commercial ends? What are ways you try to escape (and succeed in escaping!) being manipulated?

- Who and what could help you move from fear into power? *Idea 7* suggests one key is finding a "tribe" reinforcing your new insights. Discuss what this might mean to you.
- Share an empowering moment when you've learned that fear need not stop you.

Activity before next session:

- Be aware of and record fears that inhibit you and moments when you realize that you can "walk tall with fear."

CHAPTER 9: SANITY IN MOTION

As a whole group, discuss Lappé's distinction between "issues" and "entry points."

- Does it make sense?
- What other important entry points do you see now in our country or your community?

In twos or threes:

- Review *Idea 8: Living Democracy's Checklist.* Share some of the most meaningful choices you are now making to live according to your values, and apply the checklist's questions to them. Also share actions you are considering, and explore how they might fuel the positive *Spiral of Empowerment* inside the back cover.

Reconvene the whole group to discuss staying in touch as a group or in twos or threes to provide ongoing support for making the changes you desire. If participants are part of a larger group, consider:

- Choosing at least one entry point the larger group can begin acting on now and deciding how to introduce the suggestion.
- Selecting participants or a team to summarize the key lessons from this series for your larger group.

In closing, reflect as a whole group on what you have learned from *Getting a Grip,* sharing which *specific* messages you will take forward.

Also, please consider offering feedback about how to strengthen the book. I welcome suggestions and will integrate ideas from readers in future additions.

—Frances Moore Lappé
info@smallplanetinstitute.org

RECOMMENDED READING

BY THE PRINCIPALS OF THE SMALL PLANET INSTITUTE

Democracy's Edge: Choosing to Save Our Country by Bringing Democracy to Life
Frances Moore Lappé

Diet for a Small Planet
Frances Moore Lappé

Grub: Ideas for an Urban Organic Kitchen
Anna Lappé and Bryant Terry

Hope's Edge: The Next Diet for a Small Planet
Frances Moore Lappé and Anna Lappé

Surviving the Century: Facing Climate Chaos and Other Global Challenges
Edited by Herbert Girardet, with chapter by Frances Moore Lappé

World Hunger: Twelve Myths
Frances Moore Lappé, Joseph Collins and Peter Rossett, with Luis Esparza

You Have the Power: Choosing Courage in a Culture of Fear
Frances Moore Lappé and Jeffrey Perkins

AND FROM OTHERS

The Anatomy of Human Destructiveness
Erich Fromm

Earth Democracy
Vandana Shiva

The Great Turning: From Empire to Earth Community
David Korten

Hope in the Dark
Rebecca Solnit

Mindfulness
Ellen Langer

The Next Form of Democracy
Matt Leighninger

Natural Capitalism
Paul Hawken, Amory Lovins, L. Hunter Lovins

On Violence
James Gilligan

The Small-Mart Revolution: How Local Businesses Are Beating the Global Competition
Michael H. Schuman

Strong Democracy
Benjamin Barber

The Third Side
William Ury

The Web of Life
Fritjof Capra

PERIODICALS THAT OFTEN OFFER STORIES
OF LIVING DEMOCRACY

Adbusters Magazine– Canada
E-mail: info@adbusters.org
www.adbusters.org

Ode Magazine–The Netherlands
E-mail: ode@odemagazine.com
www.odemagazine.com

New Internationalist–UK
Web site: www.newint.org

Resurgence Magazine–United Kingdom
www.resurgence.org

Sojourners Magazine–USA
www.sojo.net

Utne Magazine–USA
www.utne.com

WorldWatch Magazine–USA
www.worldwatch.org/pubs/mag/

Yes! Magazine–USA
www.yesmagazine.org

WEB SITES

www.livingeconomies.org—Business Alliance for Local Living Economies

www.grist.org—Environmental News and Commentary

www.ewg.org—Environmental Working Group

www.gnn.tv—Guerrilla News Network

www.foodfirst.org—The Institute for Food and Development Policy (Food First)

www.iatp.org—Institute for Agriculture and Trade Policy

www.libertytreefdr.org—Liberty Tree Foundation for the
     Democratic Revolution

www.neweconomics.org—New Economics Foundation

www.ucsusa.org—Union of Concerned Scientists

www.wiserearth.org—Wiser Earth

www.worldchanging.org—World Changing, Change Your Thinking

www.worldfuturecouncil.org—World Future Council

ENDNOTES

1 "Suicide Prevention," World Health Organization, http://www.who.int/mental_health/prevention/suicide/suicideprevent/en/; see also, "Depression," http://www.who.int/mental_health/management/depression/definition/en/.

2 William Easterly, *The White Man's Burden* (New York: Penguin, 2006), 273.

3 Erich Fromm, *The Anatomy of Human Destructiveness* (New York: Holt, Rinehart and Winston, 1973), 149.

4 Alexis de Tocqueville, *Democracy in America*, Book I, Chapter 14, http://xroads.virginia.edu/~hyper/detoc/1_ch14.htm.

5 Jeffrey Gold, , "Wal-Mart, Toys 'R' Us Rivalry 'a Little More Cutthroat,'" *Seattle Post-Intelligencer*, November 23, 2003, Business section., http://seattlepi.nwsource.com/business/150216_toyshowdown28.html.

6 Peter Barnes, *Capitalism 3.0* (San Francisco: Berret-Koehler, 2006), 22. Calculated from annual sales of Fortune 500 corporations from data on *Fortune* magazine's Website, http://money.cnn.com/magazines/fortune/fortune500_archive/full/1955/index.htm.

7 Office for Social Justice, Archdiocese of St. Paul and Minneapolis, based on Census Bureau figures and analysis by Princeton economist Paul Krugman, http://www.osjspm.org/101_income_facts.aspx#6.

8 "CEO Pay Charts," United for a Fair Economy, http://www.faireconomy.org/research/CEO_Pay_charts.html, accessed on January 3, 2007. CEO "lunchtime" comparison: Bob Herbert, "Working for a Pittance," *The New York Times*, July 3, 2006, citing the Economic Policy Institute, Washington, D.C.

9 House Committee on Financial Services Democrats, "How Workers are Faring in the Real Bush Economy: A Report Prepared by the Democratic Staff of the House Financial Services Committee, September 22, 2006," http://financialservices.house.gov/ReportJobsWagesSept06.html

10 Paul Krugman, "The Great Wealth Transfer, "*Rolling Stone*, November 30, 2006, http://www.rollingstone.com/politics/story/12699486/paul_krugman_on_the_great_wealth_transfer.

11 Forbes Magazine, "The Richest Americans," http://www.forbes.com/lists/2006/54/biz_06rich400_The-400-Richest-Americans_land.html. $1.25 trillion total. Estimate of income of the world's poorest is based on one billion living on less than a dollar a day and three billion living on less than two dollars a day. For the world's billionaires, see: http://www.forbes.com/2007/03/07/billionaires-worlds-richest_07billionaires_cz_lk_af_0308billie_land.html
For China $2.225 trillion GDP:, see "The World Factbook," The United States Central Intelligence Agency,https://www.cia.gov/cia/publications/factbook/print/ch.html.

12 David Woodward and Andrew Sims, "Growth Isn't Working: the Unbalanced Distribution of Benefits and Costs from Economic Growth," The New Economics Foundation, http://www.neweconomics.org/gen/z_sys_publicationdetail.aspx?pid=219, 3, 17.

13 A Survey of the World Economy: More Pain than Gain, *The Economist*, September 14, 2006, 15.

14 Jeffrey Sachs, *The End of Poverty* (New York: The Penguin Press, 2005).

15 James K. Galbraith, "Mission Control," *Mother Jones*, November/December 2006, 34.

16 Bill Vorley, *Food Inc.: Corporate Concentration from Farm to Consumer*, (London: U.K. Food Group), 11.

17 For seed facts: "Global Seed Industry Concentration 2005," Communiqué Issue 90, ETC Group, September-October, 2005, 3. For media facts, see Ben Bagdikian, *The New Media Monopoly*. (Boston: Beacon Press, 2004.) *See also* Granville Williams, "The Global Network for Democratic Media," Mediachannel.org, http://www.mediachannel.org/ownership/chart.shtml. For gasoline facts, see: Public Citizen, *Mergers, Manipulation and Mirages: How Oil Companies Keep Gasoline Prices High, and Why the Energy Bill Doesn't Help*, March 2004.

18 Paul Krugman, "The Great Wealth Transfer," *Rolling Stone*, November 30, 2006, http://www.rollingstone.com/politics/story/12699486/paul_krugman_on_the_great_wealth_transfer.

19 Office for Social Justice, Archdiocese of St. Paul and Minneapolis, based on Lawrence Mishel, et al., *The State of Working America 2002/2003*, (Washington D.C.: The Economic Policy Institute, 2003), http://www.osjspm.org/101_income_facts.aspx#7.

20 Jeffrey H. Birnbaum, "The Road to Riches is Called K Street," *Washington Post*, June 22, 2005.

21 President Franklin Delano Roosevelt, speech to Congress about dangers of monopoly, April 29, 1938. http://www.presidency.ucsb.edu/ws/index.php?pid=15637

22 Tobi Mae Lippin. "Chemical Plants Remain Vulnerable to Terrorists: A Call to Action," *Environmental Health Perspectives* 114, no. 9 (2004): 114.

23 Associated Press. "U.S. food safety inspections languishing," February 26, 2007. http://fsrio.nal.usda.gov/news_article.php?article_id=4110

24 Andrew C. Revkin and Matthew Wald, "Material Shows Weakening of Climate Change Reports," *The New York Times*, http://select.nytimes.com/search/restricted/article?res=F30A10FD3C540C738E DDAA0894DF404482.

25 "Large Majorities Believe Big Companies, PACs, Media and Lobbyists Have Too Much Power and Influence in Washington," Harris Interactive, April 10, 2002, http://www.harrisinteractive.com/news/allnewsbydate.asp?NewsID=447.

26 Ori Brafman and Rod Beckstrom. *The Starfish and the Spider* (New York: Portfolio, 2007), 17-22.

27 Christopher R. Browning, *Ordinary Men: Reserve Police Battalion 101 and the Final Solution in Poland* (Harper Perennial, 1998; first published 1992), xv.

28 Ibid., xvii, 38.

29 Ibid., xv, 47.

30 Ibid., 225-26.

31 Ibid., 184-85.

32 Philip G. Zimbardo, "A Situationist Perspective on the Psychology of Evil: Understanding How Good People Are Transformed into Perpetrators," in *The Social Psychology of Good and Evil: Understanding our Capacity for Kindness and Cruelty*, ed. Arthur Miller (New York: Guilford, 2004, revised July 25, 2003), 21-50.

33 Sarah Anderson et al., "Executive Excess 2006: Defense and Oil Executives Cash in on Conflict," United or a Fair Economy, August 30, 2006, 5,http://www.faireconomy.org/reports/2006/ExecutiveExcess2006.pdf.

34 Sandra Jordan, "Old Women Step Forward as 'Martyrs,'" *The Observer*, December 12, 2006, 27.

35 Beatriz Stolowicz, "The Latin American Left: Between Governability and Change," in Daniel Chavez and Benjamin Goldfrank, eds. (London: Latin American Bureau, 2004), *The Left in the City*, citing *Desarrollo más allá de la economía*, Inter-American Development Bank, September 2000, 180.

36 Andrew Newberg and Mark Robert Waldman, *Why We Believe What We Believe: Uncovering Our Biological Need for Meaning, Spirituality, and Truth* (New York: Free Press, 2006), 8-9; Michael Bratton and Wonbin Cho, "Where is Africa Going? Views from Below, A Compendium of Trends in Public Opinion in 12 African Countries, 1999-2006," Working Paper No. 60, The Afrobarometer Network, May 2006, 17. http://www.washingtonpost.com/wp-srv/world/documents/AfropaperNo60.pdf.

37 Albert Camus, *Neither Victims Nor Executioners* (Boston: New Society Publishers, 1986), 49.

38 Thomas L. Friedman, "Time of the Turtles," *The New York Times*, August 15, 1998, A13.

39 Barry Lopez, "Imperative," *Orion*, January/February 2007, 39.

40 Stephen Breyer, *Active Liberty* (New York: Alfred Knopf, 2005), 21.

41 Marshall Sahlins, *The Use and Abuse of Biology* (Ann Arbor: University of Michigan Press, 1976), 100.

42 Michael Gurven, "To Give or Not to Give: The Behavioral Ecology of Food Transfers," *Behavioral and Brain Sciences* 27 (2004): 543-583.

43 Michael Alvard, "Good Hunters Keep Smaller Shares of Larger Pies," Open Peer Commentary, accompanying Michael Gurven, "To Give or Not to Give: The Behavioral Ecology of Food Transfers," *Behavioral and Brain Sciences* 27 (2004): 543-583.

44 Daniel Goleman, *Social Intelligence: The New Science of Human Relationships* (New York: Bantam, 2006), 57.

45 Ibid., 55.

46 Natalie Angier, "Why We're So Nice: We're Wired to Cooperate," *The New York Times,* July 23, 2002.

47 Adam Smith, *The Theory of Moral Sentiments*, ed. D.D. Raphael and A.L. Macfie (Indianapolis: Liberty Classics, 1982), pt. 2, sec. 2, ch. 3, 88.

48 Ibid., pt. 2, sec. 2, ch. 1, 80.

49 Sarah F. Brosnan and Frans B.M. de Waal, "Monkeys Reject Unequal Pay," *Nature* 423 (2003): 297-299.

50 Erich Fromm, *The Anatomy of Human Destructiveness* (New York: Holt, Rinehart and Winston, 1973), 264.

51 John J. Dinan, *The American State Constitutional Tradition* (Lawrence: University Press of Kansas, 2006), 1.

52 William H. Hastie, quoted in *The Great Quotations*, ed. George Seldes (New York: Pocketbooks, 1967), 265.

53 Gianpaolo Baiocchi, "Participation, Activism, and Politics: The Porto Alegre Experiment," in *Deepening Democracy*, ed. Archon Fung and Erik Olin Wright (New York: Verso, 2003), 47—50.

54 Gianpaolo Baiocchi, "Porto Alegre: The Dynamism of the Unorganized," in *The Left in the City*, ed. Daniel Chavez and Benjamin Goldfrank (London: Latin American Bureau, 2004), 53.

55 Gianpaolo Baiocchi, *Militants and Citizens: The Politics of Participation in Porto Alegre* (Stanford, Calif.: Stanford University Press, 2005). And personal communication, Gianpaolo Baiocchi, March 11, 2005.

56 "Beyond Red vs. Blue: Republicans Divided about Role of Government–Democrats by Social and Personal Values, Part Six," Pew Research Center, May 10, 2005, http://people-press.org/reports/display.php3?ReportID=242.

57 Laura F. Jesse, "Extra $1 million is pushed for Project Quest," *San Antonio Express-News*, August 31, 2006.

58 "Shared Decision Making at a School Site: Moving Toward a Professional Model," *American Educator* (Spring,1987): 17.

59 Janet Raloff, "Global Food Trends," *Science News* 163, no. 22 (2003), http://www.sciencenews.org/articles/20030531/food.asp.

60 Paul Hawken, Amory Lovins, and L. Hunter Lovins, *Natural Capitalism* (Boston, New York, London: Little Brown and Company, 1999), 14-15.

61 Herman Scheer, *Energy Autonomy* (Earthscan: London, Sterling, VA, 2007), 48; Cristina L. Archer and Mark Z. Jacobson, "Evaluation of Global Wind Power," Journal of Geophysical Research, Vol. 110, D12110, June 30, 2005, 1. http://www.stanford.edu/group/efmh/winds/2004jd005462.pdf.

62 Clean Elections Institute, Inc., http://www.azclean.org.

63 Micah L. Sifry and Nancy Watzman, *Is That a Politician in Your Pocket? Washington on $2 Million a Day* (Hoboken, N.J.: Wiley, 2004), 19.

64 Thomas L. Friedman, "The Power of Green," *The New York Times Magazine*, April 15, 2007, 71

65 "From Poverty to Prosperity: A National Strategy to Cut Poverty in Half," Center for American Progress, Washington, D. C., April, 2007, citing the Canadian population at 33 million, http://www.americanprogress.org/issues/2007/04/poverty_report.html.

66 Michael Myser, "Inside the $37 Billion Prison Economy," CNN Money, December 6, 2006, http://money.cnn.com/magazines/business2/business2_archive/2006/12/01/8394995/index.htm?postversion=2006120608; James J. Stephen, "State Prison Expenditures, 2001," 3, http://www.ojp.usdoj.gov/bjs/pub/pdf/spe01.pdf; for Harvard tuition 2001-2002, http://www.hsph.harvard.edu/finaid/01-02budget.shtml.

67 Harry J. Holzer et al., *The Economic Costs of Poverty in the United States: Subsequent Effects of Children Growing Up Poor* (Center for American Progress, Washington, D.C., January 2007,) 1. http://www.americanprogress.org/issues/2007/01/pdf/poverty_report.pdf

68 U.S. Environmental Protection Agency, Office of Solid Waste and Emergency Response, Technology Innovation Office, Cleaning Up the Nation's Waste Sites: Markets and Technology Trends, EPA 542-R-96-005, September 2004, http://www.clu-in.org/download/market/2004market.pdf.

69 "From Poverty to Prosperity," 8-9.

70 Dan Ackman, Corporate Taxes Continue to Plummet," first published by Forbes.com, Sept 23, 2004.

71 Paul Krugman, "Gilded Once More," *The New York Times*, April 27, 2007, A27.

72 Adam Smith, *The Wealth of Nations* (New York: Random House, 1937), bk. 5, ch. 2, pt. 2, 777.

73 Lester Brown, *Plan B 2.0*, (New York: W.W. Norton, 2006), 228-235.

74 "From Poverty to Prosperity," 5.

75 Sam Cole, "Zero Waste—On the Move Around the World: U.S. Communities, Retailers, and Other Countries Begin to Implement Producer Responsibility," Eco-Cycle, www.ecocycle.org/zero/producer.cfm.

76 Lester Brown, *Plan B 2.0*, (New York: W.W. Norton, 2006), 229.

77 Greg Anrig, Jr., "Ten Myths about Social Security," The Century Foundation, January 26, 2005, http://209.85.165.104/search?q=cache:zCjW_ZpfPvMJ:www.socsec.org/publications.asp%3Fpubi d%3D507+administrative+cost+social+security+compared+private+insurance&hl=en&gl=us&ct=c lnk&cd=5.

78 Medicare and Health Care Chartbook, Committee on Ways and Means, U.S. House of Representatives, U.S. Government Printing Office, February 27, 1997, 138, http://www.access.gpo. gov/congress/house/ways-and-means/.

79 France spends $3,159 per person with a longevity of 80.3 years, and the U.S. spent $6,102 per person in 2004 on health care with a life expectancy of 78 years. "OECD in Figures 2006-2007: Health Spending and Resources," Organization for Economic Co-operation and Development, October, 2006, http://www.oecd.org/topicstatsportal/0,2647,en_2825_495642_1_1_1_1,00.html; Martin Gaynor and Deepti Gudipati, "Health Care Costs: Do We Need a Cure," The Heinz School Review 3, no. 2 (2006).

80 "Taking on Poverty," Center for American Progress, Washington, D.C., April, 2007, http://www. americanprogress.org/issues/2007/04/poverty_event.html; for GDP per capita, see CIA World Factbook, https://www.cia.gov/library/publications/the-world-factbook/index.html.

81 These programs I learned about firsthand from the program's director Adriana Aranha on my visit to Belo Horizonte in 2000. The specifics of forty farmers and twelve thousand meals daily come from an email communication dated July 6, 2006, from Michael Jahi Chappell, mjahi@umich.edu, doctoral candidate at the University of Michigan studying Belo Horizonte.

82 Communication via email from graduate student Flavia Andrade, citing original data obtained in the official Website of the Brazilian government (www.datasus.gov.br) which shows infant mortality rate in Belo Horizonte at 15.9 per thousand in 2003; in 1993, infant mortality in Belo was 36.4/1000, http://cs.server2.textor.com/alldocs/Lansky%202.pdf.

83 See CERES, the seventeen-year-old coalition that launched the Global Reporting Initiative (GRI), the de facto international standard used by over 850 companies for corporate reporting on environmental, social, and economic performance, http://www.ceres.org; also http://www.globalreporting.org.

84 James O'Nions, "Fairtrade and Global Justice," Seedling Magazine, July 2006, http://www.grain.org/ seedling/?type=64. See also http://www.fairtrade.net and http://www.transfairusa.org.

85 Corporate Accountability International, http://www.stopcorporateabuse.org/cms/page1111.cfm.

86 "A Billion Will Die from Smoking," BBC News, October 4, 2005. quoting Professor Richard Peto, Oxford University, Oxford, England, http://209.85.165.104/search?q=cache:bUERXK7m1ygJ:news. bbc.co.uk/1/hi/health/4309222.stm+Richard+Peto,+Oxford+University+tobacco+billion&hl=en&ct =clnk&cd=6&gl=us.

87 Jack Beatty, Age of Betrayal: The Triumph of Money in America, 1865-1900 (New York: Alfred A. Knopf, 2007), 148.

88 Community Environmental Defense Fund http://www.celdf.org/PressReleases/ EastBrunswickStripsSludgeCorporationsofRigh/tabid/407/Default.aspx; Democracy Unlimited of Humboldt County, http://www.duhc.org/index.html.

89 Transcript of the PBS NOW program on this case, http://www.pbs.org/now/transcript/ transcriptNOW107_full.html.

90 Daniel McLeod, "Ballot Initiative, Democracy Unlimited: Daniel McLeod Interviews Kaitlin Sopoci-Belknap," Z Magazine Online, December 2006, http://zmagsite.zmag.org/Dec2006/mcleod1206. html.

91 Marjorie Kelly, "Holy Grail Found: Absolute, Definitive Proof That Responsible Companies Perform Better Financially," Business Ethics, Winter 2005, http://www.business-ethics.com/current_issue/ winter_2005_holy_grail_article.html.

92 Andrew W. Savitz, The Triple Bottom Line (San Francisco: Jossey-Bass, 2006), 31.

93 Daniel Gross, "Latte Laborers Take on a Latte-Liberal Business," The New York Times, April 8, 2007, Week in Review, 5.

94 "Unchaining for One Day Means Millions for Communities," American Independent Business Alliance, November 10, 2004, http://amiba.net/Unchained_national_release.html, citing "The Economic Impact of Locally Owned Businesses vs. Chains: A Case Study in Midcoast Maine," Institute for Local Self-Reliance, September 2003, http://www.newrules.org/retail/midcoaststudy.pdf.

95   The logic of this estimate: The International Cooperative Alliance reports 800 million cooperative members worldwide. Considering the combined population of the EU and the U.S. is less than this number, and assuming that at the very most half of the people in these two regions own corporate shares, one can assume as many as several hundred additional million shareholders in the rest of the world and still arrive at less than 800 million.

96   *ICA Digest*, International Cooperative Alliance, March 2007, 5, Issue 54. http://www.ica.coop/publications/digest/54-digest.pdf.

97   Examples from International Cooperative Alliance except for India, which is from: Cooperatives in Social Development, Report of the Secretary-General, United Nations General Assembly, A/60/138, July 21, 2005, 6, citing Verghese, Kurien, "India's milk revolution: investing in rural producer organizations," a paper presented at the World Bank conference "Scaling up poverty reduction: a global learning process and conference," Shanghai, May 25-27, 2004.

98   "WRC Affiliated Colleges and Universities," Workers Rights Consortium, http://www.workersrights.org/as.asp.

99   Gordon Bazemore and Maria Schiff, *Juvenile Justice Reform and Restorative Justice: Building Theory and Policy from Practice,* (Portland, Oregon: Willan Publishing, 2004), 376-378.

100 Citizens On Patrol Program (COPP), http://www.cincinnati-oh.gov/police/pages/-9496-/; *Citizen Observer*, http://www.citizenobserver.com/cov6/app/group.html?id=174.

101 Jim Giles, "Internet Encyclopaedias Go Head to Head," *Nature* 438 (December 15, 2005): 900ff.

102 Alasdair Roberts, *Blacked Out: Government Secrecy in the Information Age* (New York: Cambridge University Press, 2006), 73.

103 Archon Fung and Dara O'Rourke, "Reinventing Environmental Regulation from the Grassroots Up: Explaining and Expanding the Success of the Toxics Release Inventory," *Environmental Management* 25, no. 2 (2000): 115. http://www.archonfung.net/papers/FungORourkeTRI00.pdf.

104 Andrew W. Savitz with Karl Weber, *The Triple Bottom Line* (San Francisco: Jossey-Bass, 2006) 210.

105 United Nations Development Programme 2002, *Human Development Report 2002* (New York: Oxford University Press, 2002), 10.

106 For 12 million estimate, International Labour Organization, A Global Alliance Against Forced Labor, 2005, http://www.ilo.org/global/About_the_ILO/Media_and_public_information/Press_releases/lang-en/WCMS_005162; for 27 million and Bales, see Susan Llewelyn Leach, "Slavery is Not Dead, Just Less Recognizable, *Christian Science Monitor,* September 1, 2004, http://www.csmonitor.com/2004/0901/p16s01-wogi.html.

107 Thomas L. Friedman, "The Power of Green," *The New York Times Magazine*, April 15, 2007, 49, citing the Environmental Protection Agency.

108 *Bill Moyers Journal*, PBS, April 27, 2007.

109 Josephson Institute of Ethics, "2002 Report Card: Survey Documents Decade of Moral Deterioration: Kids Today Are More Likely To Cheat, Steal and Lie Than Kids 10 Years Ago," http://www.josephsoninstitute.org/Survey2002/survey2002-pressrelease.htm.

110 Daniel Goleman, *Social Intelligence: The New Science of Human Relationships* (New York: Bantam, 2006), 4. Citing, for the discovery of mirror neurons: G. di Pelligrino et al., "Understanding Motor Events: A Neurophysiological Study," *Experimental Brain Research* 91 (1992): 176-80.

111 Daniel Goleman, *Social Intelligence: The New Science of Human Relationships* (New York: Bantam, 2006), 4.

112 For more on the arts of democracy mentioned here, see the Small Planet Institute's downloadable document: *Doing Democracy: Ten Practical Arts*, http://democracysedge.org/handbook.pdf.

113 Benjamin Barber, "America Skips School," *Harper's Magazine*, November, 1993.

114 Jeremy Rifkin, *The European Dream: How Europe's Vision of the Future is Quietly Eclipsing the American Dream* (Cambridge: Polity Press, 2004), 48-50, 78-81.

115 Martha Meana and Lea Thaler, "Teen Sexuality and Pregnancy in Nevada," in Shalin, Dmitri, ed. *The Social Health of Nevada: Leading Indicators and Quality of Life in the Silver State* (University of Nevada, Las Vegas, 2004), http://www.unlv.edu/centers/cdclv/healthnv/teensex.html.-]

116 See the Small Planet Institute's downloadable document: *Doing Democracy: Ten Practical Arts* http://democracysedge.org/handbook.pdf.

117 See "Suggestions for Using the Believing Game," excerpted from "Conflict in Context: Understanding Local to Global Security" by Gayle Mertz and Carol Miller Lieber, Educators for Social Responsibility, 2001, http://www.esrnational.org/believinggame.htm.

118 Nancy A. Burrell, Cindy S. Zirbel, and Mike Allen, "Evaluating Peer Mediation Outcomes in Educational Settings: A Meta-Analytic Review," 21 (2003): 7-26.

119 Joseph Stiglitz, *Globalization and Its Discontents* (New York: Norton, 2003), 9.

120 Thomas L. Friedman, "Small and Smaller," *The New York Times,* March 4, 2004, A29.

121 Quoted in Dan Carney, "Dwayne's World," *Mother Jones,* July-August 1995, http://www.motherjones.com/news/special_reports/1995/07/carney.html.

122 "Power Hungry: Six Reasons to Regulate Global Food Corporations," ActionAid International, 2005, 4, http://www.actionaid.org.uk/wps/content/documents/power_hungry.pdf.

123 Nicholas D. Kristof, *"A Glide Path to Ruin,"* *The New York Times*, June 26, 2005, http://www.nytimes.com/2005/06/26/opinion/26kristof.html?ex=1277438400&en=50db1771c7550c4c&ei=5090&partner=rssuserland&emc=rss.

124 Muhammad Yunus, personal communication, July 2000, Dhaka, Bangladesh.

125 James Gilligan, *Violence: Reflections on a National Epidemic* (New York: Vintage Books/Random House, 1997), 105-107.

126 Eleanor Roosevelt, "Fear, the Great Enemy," in *You Learn by Living* (Harper & Brothers Publishers, New York, 1960), 29-30, 41.

127 Rush W. Dozier, Jr., *Fear Itself: The Origin and Nature of the Powerful Emotion That Shapes Our Lives and Our World* (New York: St. Martins, 1998), 224.

128 Aung San Suu Kyi, *Freedom from Fear* (New York: Penguin Books, 1991), 180.

129 Andrew Newberg, *Why We Believe What We Believe: Uncovering Our Biological Need for Meaning, Spirituality, and Truth* (New York: Free Press, 2006), 146.

130 Martha Stout, *The Sociopath Next Door* (New York: Broadway, 2005).

131 Thomas Jefferson in a Letter to Thomas Law, *Thomas Jefferson Writings,* ed. Merrill D. Peterson (New York: The Library of America/Liberty Classics, 1984), 337-338.

132 See, for example, the work of Marshall Rosenberg on "nonviolent communication," http://www.cnvc.org.

133 "Buying the War," *Bill Moyers Journal*, PBS, April 25, 2003.

134 "An Interview with Martha Stout," BookBrowse, http://www.bookbrowse.com/author_interviews/full/index.cfm?author_number=1097; Stanley Milgram, *Obedience to Authority: An Experimental View* (New York: HarperCollins, 1974).

135 Dee Hock, *Birth of the Chaordic Age* (San Francisco: Barrett-Koehler, 1999), 3.

136 Philip G. Zimbardo, "A Situationist Perspective on the Psychology of Evil: Understanding How Good People are Transformed into Perpetrators," in *The Social Psychology of Good and Evil: Understanding our Capacity for Kindness and Cruelty,* ed. Arthur Miller (New York: Guilford, 2004, revised July 25, 2003), 21-50.

137 Celia W. Dugger, "Even as Africa Hungers, Policy Slows Delivery of U.S. Food Aid," *The New York Times*, April 7, 2007, A1, 7.

138 Personal communication from Carolyn Dallas, Executive Director,, Time Dollar Youth Court, Washington, D.C., January 18, 2005. For more information on time-dollar-type services, contact Time Dollar Youth Court, 409 East Street N.W., Building B, Washington, DC 20001, tel. (202) 508-1612, zfowlk@cs.com, http://www.timebanks.org.

139 CoopAmerica Green Pages, http://www.coopamerica.org/pubs/greenpages/.

140 Miguel Mendonca, *Feed-In Tariffs, Accelerating the Deployment of Renewable Energy* (London: Earthscan, 2007), 45. *See also* Hermann Scheer, *Energy Autonomy*, (London: Earthscan, 2007).

141 Ibid., Mendonca, xiv.

INDEX

A

absolutism, 134
Abu Ghraib prison, 16, 17
accountability, 31, 44–46
ACORN, 82, 92
active listening, 34, 88–91
activism, 103
addiction, 111
Africa, 18, 52
agribusiness, 136
agriculture, 11
Allied Communities of Tarrant
    (ACT), 74
Alonovo.com, 143
anonymity, 134
anti-globalization, 99, 103,
    see also globalization
Apaches, 14
Applegate Partnership, 31–32
"apprentice citizenship," 62
Aranha, Adriana, 50
Archer Daniels Midland, 100
Arizona, 43, 49, 137–139
Australia, 74
Aztecs, 14

B

Bales, Kevin, 69
Barber, Benjamin, 85
Battalion 101, 15–16
Big Government, 44, 48
bin Laden, Osama, 4
biotechnology, 11
Brazil, 30, 49–50, 64, 77

Breyer, Stephen, 23
Browning, Christopher, 15
brutality, 17, 133–134
Bush administration, 47, 114, 124
Bush, George W., 4, 13, 14, 66, 122,
    124, 149
Business Alliance for Local Living
    Economies network, 60
buyers, 101–102,
    see also consumers; shopping

C

Cahn, Edgar, 140–141
California, 33–34, 54, 56–57
Camus, Albert, 21
Canada, 45, 74
capitalism, 11,
    see also market economics
Cargill, 100
celebration, 88
centralized power, 14
Chavez, Cesar, 77
chemical industry, 13
Cheney, Dick, 4
child care, 46
children, 94–96, 140–142
China, 10, 51
Chirac, Jacques, 51
citizen action, 42–43, 44–63
Citizens on Patrol
    (Cincinnati, Ohio), 63
citizenship, 103
civil rights, 12
Clean Elections movement, 43–44,
    137–139, 147, 149

climate change, 13, 49, 127–128,
    147–148
CNN, 67
Cohen, Richard, 94–95
Collins, Joe, 135
Colombia, 61
communications, 64–66
communications-knowledge
    revolution, 64–66
Communities Organized for Public
    Service (COPS), 32, 81, 89
community benefit agreements,
    53–54
community policing, 63
Community Reinvestment Act,
    81, 82
competition, 11–15
complexity, 15, 39
conflict, 88, 91–94, 120–122
Connecticut, 43
conservatives, 103
consumers, 50–51, 101–102,
    142–145,
    see also shopping
conventional farming, 103
Conversation Café, 102
Cooney, Philip, 13
CoopAmerica, 143
cooperation, 26–27
cooperative businesses, 60–61
corporate globalization, 99
corporate wealth, 9–10
corporations, 11, 12, 14–18, 37, 46,
    52–58, 98–99
Costco, 51
CostPlus, 51
Couverthié, Alma, 92–93
creative conflict, 88, 91–94
creativity, 90, 91–94, 132, 134

D

Darfur, 17, 68
Darwin, Charles, 26
de Tocqueville, Alexis, 6
dedication, 17
democracy, 6–7, 18, 21–22, 27, 28, 103
    arts of, 87–96, 153
    culture of, 86
    definition of, 6–9
    dimensions of, 42–63
    ecology of, 29–37
    experience of, 41–70
    growth of, 68
    learned, 33–34
    Living Democracy, 22–25, 27–28,
        29–37, 44, 84, 91, 95, 98, 100,
        112, 115, 123, 125, 134, 151,
        152, 153, 155
    money and, 137–139
    Thin Democracy, 9, 11–15, 14–18,
        21, 28, 44, 64, 70, 100–101,
        110, 136, 149
demonstration, 105
depression, 4
Descartes, René, 28
Didisheim, Pete, 146, 147
Donnelly, David, 139
Dozier, Rush, 120–121

E

ecological consciousness, 69–70
ecology, 69–70
economic growth, 10–11
economic power, 50–51
Economist, The, 11
education, 48
Education for Sustainable Living
    Program, 33–34
Edwards, John, 65
Einstein, Albert, 130

Elbow, Peter, 89–90
elections, 8
electronic waste, 145–147
Ellsberg, Daniel, 65–66
empathy, 27, 123
empowerment, 34–35, 37, 137,
    150–151, 153,
    see also power
Encyclopedia Britannica, 65
entitlement programs, 48
entry points, 136–150, 150
environment, the, 45, 46–47, 49, 66,
    see also pollution
Environmental Protection Agency,
    45, 58
ethics, 74–75
Europe, 47, 68, 74,
    see also specific countries
European Court of Human Rights, 68
evaluation, 88
evil, 4, 17, 133
extremism, 17–18

F

fair-labor practices, 62
fair trade, 99–101, 149
Fair Trade economy, 51
Fair Trade movement, 143, 144–145
fairness, 28
fear, 4, 118, 119–122, 123, 124,
    127, 153
"feed-in tariff" (FIT), 148–149
Feinstein, Harold, 155
Finland, 60
Florida, 51
food, 3, 13, 38, 49–50, 58, 61, 62,
    68, 113–114, 135–136
food aid, 135–136
Food First (Institute for Food and
    Development Policy), 135

food industry, 13, 58, 61
food shortages, 113–114
fossil fuels, 148
frames, 97–98, 153
"frames of orientation," 6, 18
France, 49, 51, 86
Franklin, Benjamin, 22, 130
free markets, 99–101
free trade, 104
Freire, Paulo, 92
Friedman, Thomas, 21, 44, 98
Fromm, Erich, 6, 28

G

Galbraith, James, 11
Gandhi, Mohandas Karamchand, 5
Garijo, Esteban, 149
gasonline, 11
GE. *see* General Electric
General Electric, 57–58
General Motors, 10
genetically modified agriculture, 11
genocide, 68
George Washington University,
    144–145
Germany, 64, 74–75, 86, 148
Gilligan, James, 110–111
global corporate power, 98–99
global heating, 147
Global Tobacco Treaty (2003),
    52, 67
global warming. see global heating
globalization, 98–99, 104
GM. *see* General Motors
Goleman, Daniel, 27, 76
goodness, 25–29
Goodwyn, Lawrence, 97
Gore, Al, 127–128
government, 8, 44–50
Green Basket program (Brazil), 50

green energy, 147–150
Green, Stephanie Faith, 144–145
Gross, Matthew, 65
Gurven, Michael, 27

H

Hastie, William, 29
Hawken, Paul, 67
health care, 46, 48–49
Hobbes, Thomas, 6
Hock, Dee, 129
Holocaust, the, 15–16
Home Depot, 52
human dignity, 67–69
human nature, xiv, 15–17, 25–29, 39,
    74–75, 132
human rights, 48–49, 67–69
human trafficking, 68–69
humility, 18–19, 152, 154
Hundt, Karen, 80
hunger, 3
Hussein, Saddam, 4

I

idealism, 17
ideas, xiv, 5–6
ideology, 134
Immelt, Jeffrey, 57
imprintability, 76
Inca, 14
income gap, 10, 12
Independent Media Center, 67
India, 61
Industrial Areas Foundation, 81, 83
"Indymedia", 67
information, 64–66
Institute for Food and Development
    Policy (Food First), 135
International Co-operative Alliance, 60

International Criminal Court, 68
International Forum on
    Globalization, 99
International Monetary Fund, 99
Internet, the, 67
invest-with-social-purpose movement,
    50–51
investors, 50–51
Iowa, 93
Iowa Citizens for Community
    (Iowa CCI), 93–94
Iraq, U.S. war in, 14, 16, 17, 86, 124
Ireland, 49
Iroquois Confederacy, 22
issues, 136
Italy, 61

J

Janis-Aparicio, Madeline, 53–54
Japan, 74
J.C. Penney's, 51
Jefferson, Thomas, 22, 123
Just Harvest, 114
just6dollars.org, 43

K

Kansas, 41–42
Kentuckians for the Commonwealth
    (KFTC), 82
Kentucky, 82
Kenya, 76
KIDS Consortium (Maine), 62
knowing, 154–155
knowledge, 64–66
Krishnamurti, Jiddu, 126
Kuwait, 61

L

labeling, 134
labor laws, 12, 51
Landay, Jonathan, 124
Landless Workers' Movement
    (Brazil), 77
language, 97–105
Lappé, Anna, 119, 132–133
Lappé, Frances Moore, 119, 126,
    132–133, 152
Latin America, 17–18
law enforcement, 63
Lawrence CommunityWorks
    (Massachusetts), 92
League of Women Voters, 137
Leave Us Alone Coalition, 26
liberals, 104
Linux, 64–65
listening, 88–91
Listening Project
    (North Carolina), 90
Living Democracy, 22–25, 27–28, 44,
    84, 91, 95, 98, 100, *112*, 115, 123,
    125, 134, 151, 152, 155
        dynamism of, 29–31
        ecology of, 29–37
Living Democracy Checklist, 153
        qualities of, 29–37
        values-guided, 31–33
lobbyists, 12–13
local economies, 59–60
local food movements, 62
"local living economies", 59–60
Los Angeles Alliance for a New
    Economy, 53–54
Los Angeles International Airport, 53

M

Maathai, Wangari, 76–77
Mackey, John, 58

Maggie, Lizzie, 9–10, 12, 37
Maine, 43, 47, 49, 62, 139, 145–147
Manteris, Willie, 121
Margulies, Anne, 64
market economics, 6, 8, 9–12,
    see also capitalism
Massachusetts, 81, 82, 92
Massachusetts Institute of
    Technology, 64
materialism, 8, 17
Maxxam, 56–57
MBNA, 51
McCoy, Martha, 41–42
McDonald's, 51, 142
Mead, Marge, 137–139
meaning, 17–18, 21, 28
media, 11
mediation, 34, 88, 94–96
Medicaid, 48
Medicare, 48
Mendonca, Miguel, 148–149
mentoring, 34, 88
Merrimack Valley Project
    (Massachusetts), 82
Metro Alliance, 32
Microsoft, 64
Mine-Ban Treaty (1997), 67
minimum wage, 12, 46, 49, 104
Minnesota, 82
mirror neurons, 75–76
MIT. *see* Massachusetts Institute of
    Technology
money, 137–139
Monopoly, 9, 10
Monsanto, 11
Moore, Margaret, 73, 74
movies, 11
Moyers, Bill, 73
Musayev, Lina, 144–145
mutual accountability, 31

N

Najar, Fatima, 17–18
National Coalition for Dialogue and
    Deliberation, 102
national debt, 104
National Green Pages, 143
National People's Action, 81
Natural Resources Council
    of Maine, 146
Nature magazine, 65
negotiation, 34, 88
networking, 67
neuroscience, 75–76
New York, 42–43, 54, 82
New York Times, 66
Newberg, Andrew, 19, 132
Njoya, Timothy, 119–120, 126
No Taxpayer Money for Politicians
    (Arizona), 139
nonprofit organizations, 104
Norquist, Grover, 25–26
North American Free Trade
    Agreement (NAFTA), 100
North Carolina, 90

O

Ohio, 82–83
one-rule economics, 9–11, 12, 17, 21,
    98–99, 100, 132
O'Neill, Paul, 66
"open course ware," 64
open markets, 11–15
open source, 64
organic farming, 104
Organic Valley, 61
O'Rourke, Patrick, 35
Oxfam America, 144

P

Parker Brothers, 9
participatory budgeting, 30–31
Pastors for Peace, 121
Pennsylvania, 55–56
Pentagon Paper, 65–66
Perkins, Jeffrey, 126
plenty, 38–39
Poder Institute, 92
political imagination, 88
politics, warping of, 12–13
pollution, 45–46, 66, 69, 79–80,
    145–147. *see also* environment, the
poverty, 3, 11, 45, 46, 47, 49
power, 5, 9, 14, 17, 34–35, 37,
    42–43, 73–84, 110, 134, 153, *see
    also* empowerment; powerlessness
    art of, 85–96
relational power, 78–83
power shopping, 142–145, 149
powerlessness, 5, 14, 17, 83, 110,
    137, 149,
    see also power
pro-choice movement, 104
pro-life movement, 104
problem solving, 28
producer responsibility, 45, 47,
    145–147
protest, 105
public dialogue, 88
public judgment, 88
public life, 36, 105
publishing, 11

Q

QUEST (Quality Employment
    Through Skills Training), 32–33

R

Rainforest Action Network, 52
Reagan, Ronald, 8, 44, 48
realism, 124
recycling, 145–147
reflecting, 34
reflection, 88
regulation, 101, 105
rejection, 117–118
relational power, 78–83
renewables, 147–148
Riggs, Sally, 93–94
Right-to-Know laws, 66
Roosevelt, Eleanor, 115
Roosevelt, Franklin Delano, 13
Russia, 17
Rwanda, 17

S

Sachs, Jeffrey, 11
sacrifice, 17
Sahlins, Marshall, 26
Saludcoop (Colombia), 61
same-sex marriage, 105
sanity, 130
scarcity, 7–8, 21, 38–39, 64,
    113–114, 131–132
Scheer, Hermann, 39
School Mediation Associates
    (Massachusetts), 94–95
scorecard.org, 66
SEC, 51
Shelby County Interfaith
    Organization (Memphis,
    Tennessee), 82
Shipley, Jack, 31–32
shopping, 142–145,
    see also buyers; consumers
Simpson, Deb, 139
slavery, 68–69

Small Planet Institute, 133
Smith, Adam, 27, 28, 46
social justice, 104
social modeling, 16
Social Security, 12, 48
solar energy, 148–149
South Mountain Company, 81
Soviet Union, collapse of the, 85
Spain, 148–149
Spiral of Empowerment, 37–39, 98,
    137, 150, 151
Spiral of Powerlessness, 6, 7, 37, 110,
    137, 142–143, 149
Stallman, Richard, 64–65
standards, 101
Staples Center (Los Angeles), 53
Starbucks, 51
Stédile, João Pedro, 77
Stiglitz, Joseph, 98
Stoneman, Dorothy, 141–142
Stout, Martha, 125
Strobel, Warren, 124
students, 62
Study Circles Resource Center,
    41–42, 102
Sudan, 68
suicide bombers, 17–18
Sun City Democratic Club, 137
sustainability, 153
Sustainable Connections, 59–60
Suu Kyi, Aung San, 122, 123
Sweden, 47, 60
Switzerland, 60

T

Tanzania, 18
Target, 51
Tate & Lyle, 100
tax shifting, 47
taxes, 46, 47, 105

Teen Courts, 140–141
Tennessee, 76–77, 82
Texas, 32, 74, 81, 89, 149
"The Believing Game," 89–90
Thin Democracy, 9, 11–15, 14–18,
    21, 28, 44, 64, 70, 100–101, 110,
    136, 149
Thompson, Seymour D., 55
Time Dollars, 140–141, 149
Tobacco industry, 52
transparency, 66
trust, 86–87

U

Union of Consumer Co-operative
    Societies (Kuwait), 61
United Kingdom, 51
United States, 10, 45, 48, 49, 51, 74,
    86, *see also specific states*
United Steel Workers, 114
United Students for Fair Trade, 144

V

values, 31–33
Van der Hoff, Frans, 51
Vietnam, war in, 65–66
Vision 2000 (Chattanooga,
    Tennessee), 79–80
Viveret, Patrick, 117

W

Wal-Mart, 10, 56–57
War on Poverty, 46
Washington, 47, 59, 149
waste, 38
wealth, 9–11
Welch, Jack, 57
welfare state, 105
Whole Foods Market, 58

Wikipedia, 65
wind energy, 149
Winslade, Aurora, 34
Wisconsin, 54, 61, 149
wiserearth.org, 67
Worker's Party (Brazil), 30
workers' rights, 12
Working Families Party (New York),
    42–43
World Business Council for
    Sustainable Development, 57
World Economic Forum, 60
World Health Organiztion, 4, 52
World Social Forum, 99
World Trade Organization, 67, 99

Y

Youth Action Program, 82
YouthBuild, 82, 141–142, 149
Yunus, Muhammad, 109, 113

Z

"Zero Hunger" campaign (Brazil), 50
Zimbardo, Philip, 16

OTHER CURRENT TITLES FROM MEMBERS OF THE SMALL PLANET INSTITUTE TEAM

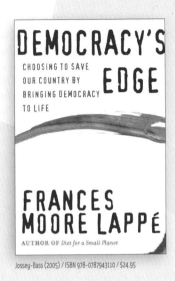

Jossey-Bass (2005) / ISBN 978-0787943110 / $24.95

Democracy's Edge
Choosing to Save Our Country
by Bringing Democracy to Life
by Frances Moore Lappé

"Lappé is a pioneer in democratic thought and action. Democracy's Edge exemplifies her path-blazing role in keeping democracy alive in our time." —CORNEL WEST, Princeton University

"There is a small number of people in every generation who are forerunners, in thought, action, spirit, who swerve past the barriers of greed and power to hold a torch high for the rest of us. Frances Moore Lappé is one of those." —HOWARD ZINN

Tarcher (2006) / ISBN: 978-1585424597 / $18.95

Grub
Ideas for an Urban Organic Kitchen
by Anna Lappé, Bryant Terry, Foreword by Eric Schlosser

"... ingenious ..." —The New York Times

"Every movement needs its revolutionaries and spokespersons, and in the growing crusade for a healthy, ethical, and 'fair' food system, Bryant Terry and Anna Lappé happen to be both." — SOJOURNERS MAGAZINE

Ask your favorite bookseller or visit www.smallplanetinstitute.org

OTHER CURRENT TITLES FROM MEMBERS OF THE SMALL PLANET INSTITUTE TEAM

FRANCES MOORE LAPPÉ and ANNA LAPPÉ

Tarcher (2003) / ISBN: 978-1585422371 / $14.95

Hope's Edge
The Next Diet for a Small Planet
by Frances Moore Lappé, Anna Lappé

"Absolutely one of the most important books as we move further in the 21st century."
—JANE GOODALL

"Hope's Edge is not only a brilliant analysis of the global food and hunger challenge; it is also a philosophical work of the first order."
—GEORGE MCGOVERN, UN Global Ambassador for Hunger

"Passionate and wise ... Just the book we need now."   —ERIC SCHLOSSER, author of Fast Food Nation

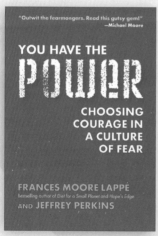

Tarcher (2005) / ISBN: 978-1585424245 / $13.95

You Have the Power
Choosing Courage in a Culture of Fear
by Frances Moore Lappé, Jeffrey Perkins

"Outwit the fearmongers. Read this gutsy gem!"
—MICHAEL MOORE

"... exhilarating jujitsu of a book ... liberating stuff."   —STUDS TERKEL

"Challenging the 'official word' that has proclaimed fear an essential attribute of patriotism, Lappé... and Perkins share portraits of extraordinary, ordinary people who have overcome their personal fears."
—Library Journal

Ask your favorite bookseller or visit www.smallplanetinstitute.org